TRAMPING IN FIORDLAND

TRAMPING IN FIORDLAND

THE MOST POPULAR TRACKS IN NEW ZEALAND'S
SOUTH-WEST WILDERNESS

MARIOS GAVALAS

NH

NEW
HOLLAND

First published in 2007 by New Holland Publishers (NZ) Ltd
Auckland · Sydney · London · Cape Town

218 Lake Road, Northcote, Auckland 0627, New Zealand
Unit 1, 66 Gibbes Street, Chatswood, NSW 2067, Australia
86–88 Edgware Road, London W2 2EA, United Kingdom
80 McKenzie Street, Cape Town 8001, South Africa

www.newhollandpublishers.co.nz

Publishing manager: Matt Turner
Design, editing and project management: Alison Dench
Cover design: Gina Hochstein
Maps: Nick Keenleyside; base relief work by Geographx

National Library of New Zealand Cataloguing-in-Publication Data

Gavalas, Marios, 1973-
Tramping in Fiordland : the most popular tracks in New Zealand's
south-west wilderness / author and photographer,
Marios Gavalas.
Includes bibliographical references and index.
ISBN 978-1-86966-153-3
1. Trails—New Zealand—Fiordland—Guidebooks.
2. Fiordland (N.Z.)—Guidebooks. I. Title.
796.51099396—dc 22

Colour reproduction by Pica Digital Pte Ltd, Singapore
Printed by Times Offset (M) Sdn Bhd, Malaysia, on paper sourced from sustainable
forests.

10 9 8 7 6 5 4 3 2 1

CONTENTS

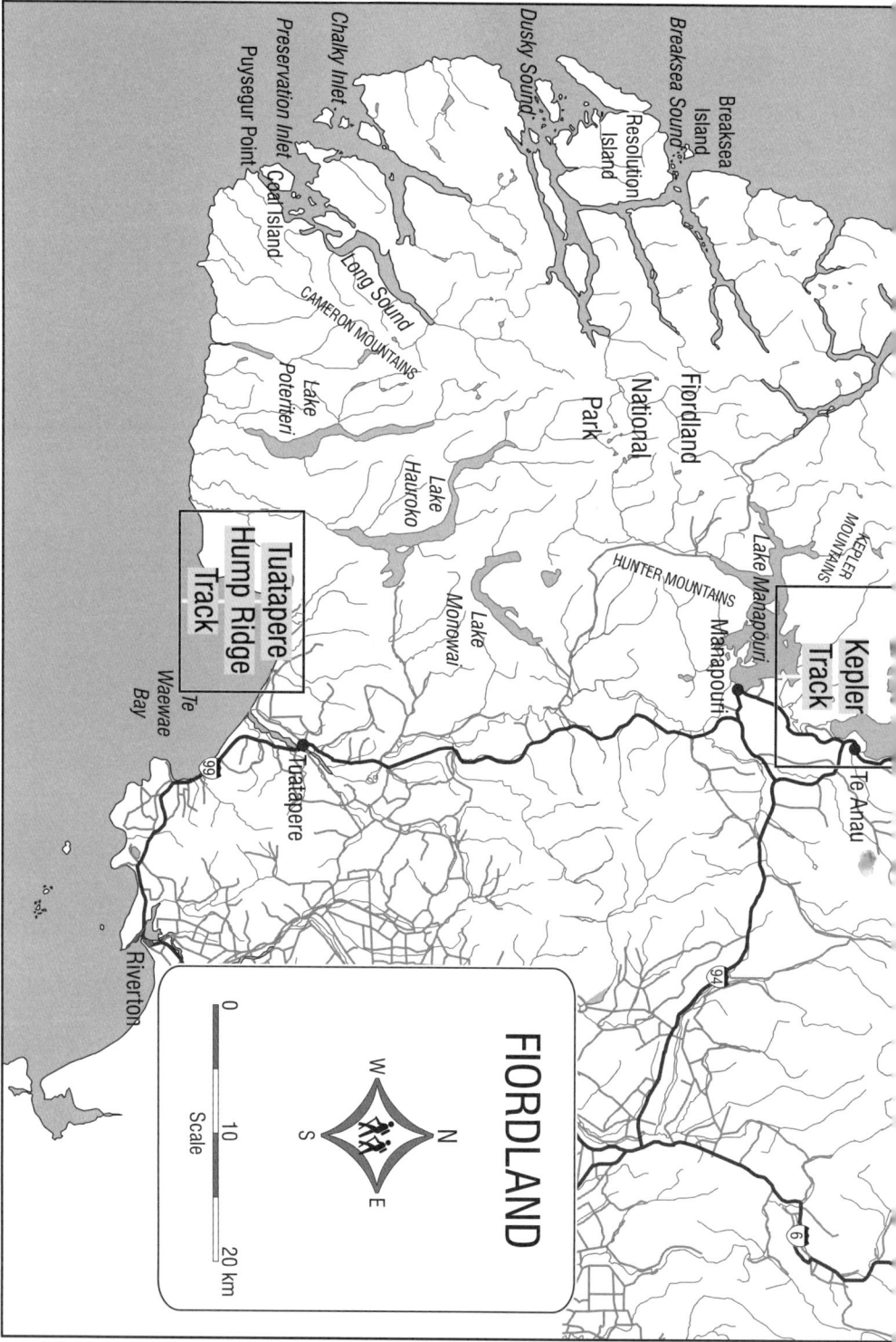

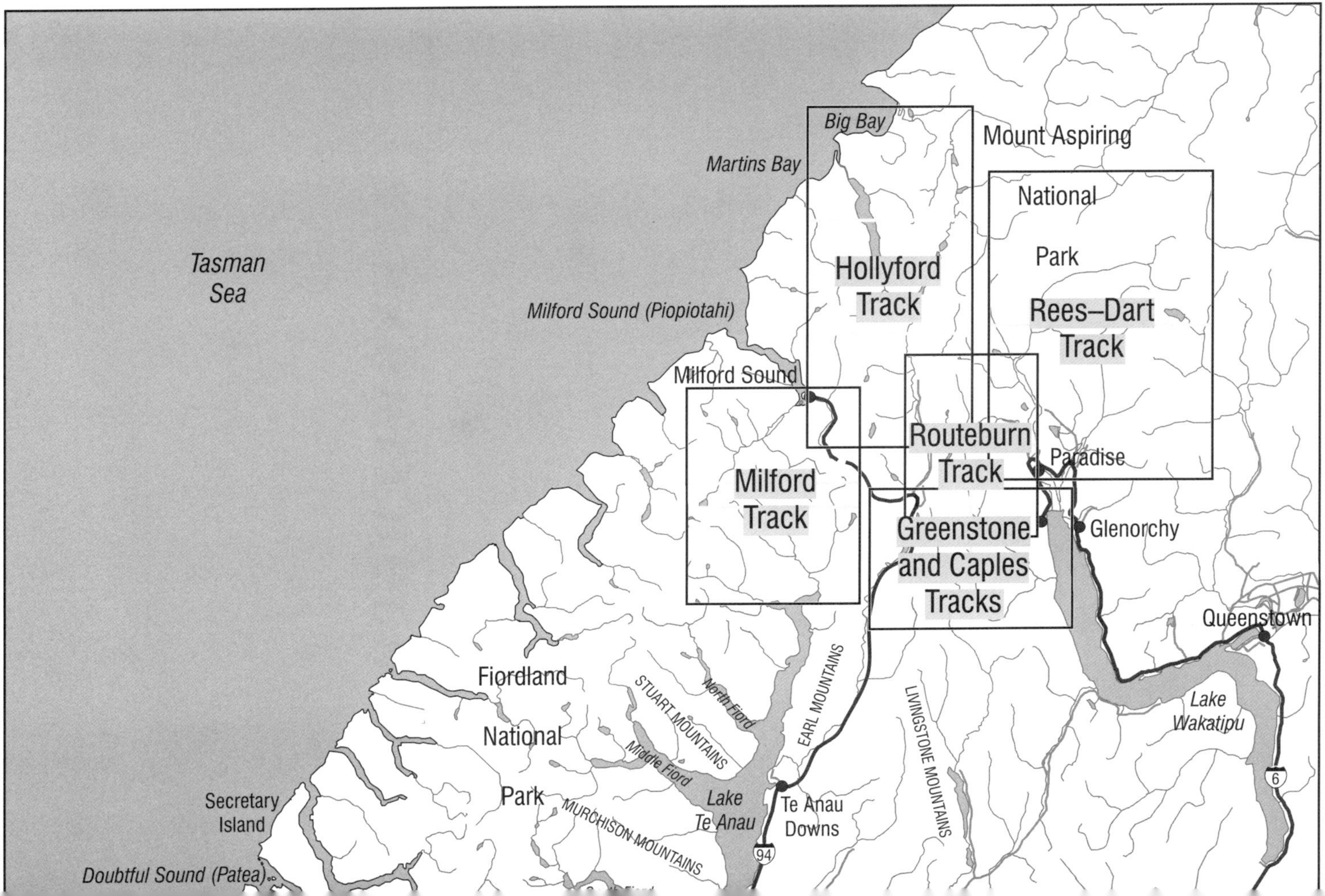

Tasman
Sea

Doubtful Sound (Patea)

Secretary
Island

Fiordland

National

Park

MURCHISON MOUNTAINS

Te Anau

Lake
Te Anau

94

Te Anau
Downs

EARL MOUNTAINS

LIVINGSTONE MOUNTAINS

Middle Fiord

STUART MOUNTAINS

North Fiord

Milford Sound (Piopiotahi)

Milford Sound

Martins Bay

Milford
Track

Hollyford
Track

Big Bay

Mount Aspiring

Greenstone
and Caples
Tracks

Routeburn
Track

National

Park

Rees–Dart
Track

Paradise

Glenorchy

Lake
Wakatipu

Queenstown

6

ACKNOWLEDGEMENTS

Thanks to my family for their support, enduring an absent husband and father. Staff at Department of Conservation Te Anau, including Ross Kerr, Caroline Carter and Odette Singleton, have been supportive of the project, while visitor centre staff were always cheerful in the face of constant requests. My appreciation to Alison Dench and Matt Turner at New Holland for seeing the project to completion. Peter Johnson has enlightened me about the forest world and in a roundabout way brought me to Fiordland. While some tramps were researched solo, on others I shared good company and experiences with friends and family. Cheers to Guy, Annika, Peter and Warren, who accompanied me during the research.

PREFACE

S ome cultures call it hiking, others trekking, walking or backpacking. In New Zealand we call it tramping. It's only natural tramping should be so widely embraced here, where there are more opportunities to enjoy unrivalled scenery than any other country of equivalent size. And Fiordland, with its dramatic concentration of mountains and valleys, lush impenetrable forest, wild coastline and a surprising catalogue of human endeavours, is at the top of just about every tramper's wish list.

The grandeur of Fiordland has a way of getting under your skin. As a tramper and guide, I have often been asked which is the best track in the region. The question may as well be 'Who of your children is the favourite?' or 'What's the best song ever written?' A straight answer is impossible. All tracks have their virtues. The Tuatapere Hump Ridge Track's tors and tarns, the Kepler's lakes, the Milford's long historical legacy, the Hollyford's journey from the mountains to the sea, the Routeburn's unparalleled views, the Greenstone and Caples Tracks' echo of Maori pathways or the glaciers of the Rees–Dart? Make your own judgement and enjoy the journey involved in coming to your conclusion.

There are plenty of tramping books on New Zealand, but most are inventories of tracks, with brief notes designed to help you select the best tramps before embarking on your travels. *Tramping in Fiordland* is different. This is one to stick in the top pocket of your pack and read as you take a break at the end of each section. Along the way, you'll learn about the geological, natural and human histories embedded in the landscapes you are walking through.

As a geography student in England (many years ago), my knowledge of Fiordland was confined to the pages of academic texts. It was bloody boring. Now that I tramp through these landscapes, and my senses and emotions are engaged, Fiordland has become real and I have developed a passion for the place. I hope reading *Tramping in Fiordland* will be the first step in a similar transformation for you.

As one of the last true wilderness areas of planet Earth, Fiordland deserves respect. Help in its preservation. Keep small, tread lightly and appreciate its uniqueness.

Marios Gavalas

HOW THE LAND
WAS FORMED

The fiords, mountains, glaciers, valleys, lakes and coast of Fiordland are awe-inspiring to all, but the story of how they came to be is only just beginning to be told. Isolation, rugged terrain, sandflies, unpredictable weather, sparsity of settlement and geological complexity have until recently deterred geologists from studying the region at first hand.

THE GEOLOGY OF FIORDLAND

Finds of graptolite fossils have dated the slaty mudstones around Chalky and Preservation Inlets as some of the oldest in New Zealand, at around 450 million years old. Most of Fiordland's basement rocks were laid down while New Zealand was on the south-eastern rim of Gondwanaland, an amalgamation of Antarctica, Australia, Africa, India, South America and New Zealand. The characteristic rocks of Fiordland were eroded off a volcanic arc on the edge of the vast ancestral land mass then compressed and heated to become schist, gneiss and orthogneiss.

Between 300 million and 100 million years ago intrusive plutonic rocks, such as the hard granitic diorite and gabbro of the Darrans and around Milford Sound, bubbled up between these basement rocks. This rock is relatively unbroken with faults and fractures, which means the steep valley sides are retained, and the ranges and peaks remain higgledy-piggledy, with little constancy in the grain.

Around 30 million years ago global climates were warmer than today. Sea levels were substantially higher and the nascent New Zealand land mass exhibited lower relief. Fiordland was effectively an island and the limestones of the eastern ranges around Te Anau were formed. The Alpine Fault also developed around this time, with the Te Anau and Waiau Basins forming from movement along fault lines. The Alpine Fault is the major line of tectonic movement in New Zealand and defines the country's landscape. It emerges above sea level at John O'Groats River just north of Milford Sound, then weaves over the Hollyford Valley before commencing its journey up the spine of the South Island. In the Fiordland area, the Australian Plate is being subducted beneath the Pacific Plate and the collision has formed the Fiordland mountains and the Southern Alps.

Over the last 5 million years there has been around 10 mm of uplift per year, a veritable hare's pace in geological terms – in fact this is one of the most dynamic plate boundaries on the planet. Sometimes the movement occurs in frightening jumps of up to 8 horizontal metres and 12 vertical metres at a time. Imagine the earthquakes associated with something like this! The most dramatic illustration of these long-term movements can be found in the Red Hills just north of the Hollyford Valley and the Dun Mountains in Nelson, both of which have an unusual ultramafic rock with high concentrations of manganese and iron. The two ranges, now 480 km apart, were once joined but the Alpine Fault has bisected them and slowly nudged them apart.

THE WORK OF THE GLACIERS

There are few places on the planet where the effects of the glacial episodes of the last 2 million years are so dramatically displayed as they are in Fiordland. In the Otiran glaciation between 80,000 and 10,000 years ago the ice over Fiordland was up to 2 km deep. All but the highest peaks were covered and massive glaciers charged over and through everything that lay in their paths. U-shaped valleys carved during earlier glaciations were deepened and their form accentuated – Milford Sound and the Eglinton Valley are apt examples of this distinctive U profile.

Many other landscape features are witness to the work of glaciers. Where two glaciers were separated by a ridge this became chiselled to a sharp edge known as an arête. The Kepler Track between Mt Luxmore and the descent to the Iris Burn is a good example. And as the weight of ice scoured the head of a valley it created a bowl shape in the rock called a cirque, seen at valley heads such as Iris Burn.

Where a tributary glacier met a deeper main valley glacier a hanging valley was left behind. When the glaciers melted, the hanging valleys were left perching above the main valley. These are well illustrated on the Darrans, on the far side of the valley to the Hollyford Track. Before glaciation, many river valleys had interlocking spurs protruding into the valley floor. The glaciers had no regard for these obstructions, tearing through the rock and truncating the spurs to leave a triangular face bisecting the former ridgeline. These are best seen on the Lake McKerrow section of the Hollyford Track.

The Kepler and Greenstone Tracks both have excellent examples of another glacial feature, the *roche moutonnée*. These elongated rock outcrops have a gentle, smooth slope on the upstream side and a rougher, steeper slope on the downstream side. They are formed where a glacier scours the outcrop on the up side and plucks rocks away on the down side.

The centre of the glacier encounters less resistance than the edges, so it flows faster. This sets up a series of internal currents, which run to the centre, carrying rock up towards the surface. When the glacier melts, this accumulation of rock is left behind in an upturned V shape called a kame. Kame terraces are deposits of lateral moraine dumped at a time when the glacier's level was constant. There are examples of both kames and kame terraces on the route to Cascade Saddle on the Rees–Dart Track.

Lakes Te Anau and Manapouri are also glacially sculpted. Vast quantities of glacially eroded material were transported from the mountains and deposited in the basins as huge outwash plains. The moraines and outwash gravels have left a series of terraces around the lakes that are now the prize of property developers.

At the height of glaciation, sea levels were as much as 120 m lower than they are today and the ice reached over 10 km out from today's shoreline. Stewart Island was joined to the South Island. The Waitutu marine terraces, seen from the Hump Ridge Track, are a physical imprint of the changes in sea level over millions of years. The 13 terraces rise to 1000 m above sea level and stretch 12 km inland from the south coast between Te Waewae Bay and Lake Hakapoua. The rise and fall of sea levels associated with glacial episodes is visible in the varied erosion height at the coast, and this effect has been compounded by the tectonic uplift of the land mass. The last three terraces were formed in the last interglacial, 120,000 to 80,000 years ago.

Although most of the glaciers have gone, the fine craftsmanship of the elements continues. Fiordland's legendary rainfall feeds watercourses that, when in flood, are powerful enough to move boulders the size of a truck, and the rivers, streams and creeks are still shaping the landscape. Fiordland is very much a work in progress.

A WORLD OF GREEN

F iordland's forests have many secrets. The innumerable hues of green, the entwining lattice of vines, mantle of moss and luxuriance of the foliage fools many trampers into feeling they are in a tropical jungle. The rain-soaked forests give way to alpine plants at higher altitudes. Above the treeline these alpine gardens are filled with highly specialised and hardy plants, well adapted to the extreme conditions.

FIORDLAND FORESTS

The dominant forest type in Fiordland is beech. These trees have close relatives in South America, Australia, New Caledonia and New Guinea – and fossil evidence has been found in Antarctica – indicating the family dates back nearly 100 million years to the time when New Zealand was part of Gondwanaland, the ancestral land mass for the southern hemisphere continents.

Silver beech (*Nothofagus menziesii*), with its white or silvery bark, is the most widespread. It can grow to 25 m tall and compete in the canopy with podocarps. At the treeline, between 850 m and 1000 m, it is ubiquitous and takes on a stunted form, dripping with moss or old man's beard (*Usnea* lichen). Clipped by the howling winds, stunted by a cool growing season and deprived of sunlight by the prevalence of cloud, these gnarled, twisted trees grow in stands sometimes known as goblin forests. Red beech (*Nothofagus fusca*) grows on more fertile sites, while mountain beech (*Nothofagus solandri* var. *cliffortioides*) tolerates both drier conditions and shallow infertile soils.

On the trunks of many specimens grow large wart-like galls caused by a fungus. The soft fruiting bodies resemble golf balls and may lie sprinkled on the ground below the trees. They are sometimes referred to as 'beech strawberries'.

The beech's method of seed dispersal is rather rudimentary – a seed drops from the tree and lands where it lands. Unsurprisingly this slows the advance of a beech forest. As seedlings also depend on a mycorrhizal fungus that lives only on the roots of adult beech trees, young trees cannot survive far from their family. Once established in Fiordland, however, the beeches leave little room for other trees, save a few podocarps at lower altitudes.

The genus for the southern beeches is *Nothofagus*, or false beech. Classifying plants was not an easy task for the early European botanist/explorers, and they tended to describe plants according to their northern hemisphere counterparts. On Cook's voyages, *Nothofagus* specimens were collected from South America, Australia and New Zealand. These were later described by Sir W. J. Hooker, director of the Royal Botanic Gardens at Kew in the 1840s, as beech. In 1850, a Dutch botanist, C. L. Blume, managed to separate the northern from the southern beeches, conferring the name *Nothofagus* on the southern genus.

In addition to the beeches, there are podocarps in the mix of Fiordland's forests. The podocarps are a family of cone-bearing trees with a lineage stretching back more than 200 million years. They evolved before the appearance of flowering plants and are distinguished by a succulent foot-like appendage on the seed. This gives rise to the term podocarp (foot seed). The fleshy fruits are carried by native birds, including kaka, kereru and tui. The podocarps mainly occupy the fertile deep soils of valley floors or the heads of fiords. Notable species encountered in Fiordland are rimu and kahikatea.

STARTING FROM SCRATCH

In Fiordland's extreme conditions, slips regularly peel off the precipitous hillsides in huge triangles. The debris accumulates as fans and the process of regeneration begins. First to recolonise the thin soils of slip faces are tutu (*Coriaria arborea*) or manuka (*Leptospermum scoparium*). Wineberry (*Aristotelia serrata*), tree fuchsia (*Fuchsia excorticata*) and putaputa-weta (*Carpodetus serratus*) are also pioneers on the jumbled rock and soil. Mountain ribbonwood (*Hoheria lyallii*) likes the deeper soils of upland fans.

A glance at exposed areas of rock disturbed by a slip or on the edges of streams gives a good indication of the succession of plant life that recolonises bare rock. On the bottom rung are lichens, able to colonise bare surfaces where no other life can survive. Lichens lie low to the wind, derive nutrients from the rock and hibernate in a torpid state without water. Lichens are symbiotic associations between fungi and algae. The fungi provide a home for the algae, which manufacture food from sunlight.

The crustose lichens that mottle the bare rocks with colourful adornments are able to secrete an acid which eats into the rock and helps to create the embryonic soils for higher plants to exploit. Weathering agents such as frost, rain and sun also release minerals from the rock, freeing up the nutrients essential for higher plant life. Enter the bryophytes, the mosses and liverworts that are one of the most startling features of Fiordland's forest. Shrouding every surface in a mantle of greens, reds and browns, these delicate plants provide a cushion for raindrops, reducing their erosive powers. By locking in moisture they also maintain a humid forest interior, providing suitable conditions and seed beds for other plants to germinate. As the higher plants die and decay, the bryophytes trap the litter and organic acids, allowing the development of deeper soils.

Rimu (*Dacrydium cupressinum*), a handsome tree, can live for over a thousand years. Its drooping branchlets and archaic foliage impart an ancient feel to the tree – you could easily imagine dinosaurs browsing on the prickly leaves. Rimu is the most widespread of all New Zealand forest trees, occurring throughout the North, South, and Stewart Islands from lowland to montane forest. The hard timber has a rich red colour and an attractive grain.

Kahikatea (*Dacrycarpus dacrydioides*), or white pine, likes wet feet and dense stands thrust skywards in raggedy unison on swampy lowland sites. It is the tallest native tree (up to 50 m high) with a trunk as straight as a mast. Its absence of a tainting odour made it the favoured timber to make butter cases for export.

Among the fern species present are tree ferns. *Cyathea medullaris* or mamaku is the largest, its skirt of dead fronds hindering the adhesion of epiphytes. These fronds were used by Maori and early pioneers to make mattresses. *Cyathea smithii* or soft tree fern, also known as whe, is common, as is *Dicksonia squarrosa* or slender tree fern (wheki). These stand like sentries in moist gullies.

Ground ferns are abundant, and the eastern forests of Fiordland are largely dominated by crown fern (*Blechnum discolor*). Other common ground ferns include kiokio (*Blechnum novae-zelandiae*), hen and chicken fern (*Asplenium bulbiferum*), where the new growth perches on the old fronds, and prickly shield fern (*Polystichum vestitum*), named for the texture of the fronds. Epiphytic filmy ferns are a conspicuous shroud on many forest trees and shrubs and also abound on the forest floor. The most common are the delicate *Hymenophyllum* species and the kidney fern *Trichomanes reniforme*, which grows up tree trunks like gaiters.

A closer examination of ferns reveals spore-producing bodies (sporangia) on the underside of the fronds. They are usually clustered in spore cases known as sori. These spores are the asexual reproductive part of the fern and are dispersed by the wind to germinate into a gametophyte, a moss-like plant at a different phase in the life cycle. The gametophyte contains male and female sex organs, and the moist forest conditions allow a small sperm to swim and fertilise the female. These grow into another fern plant.

The composition of smaller plants in Fiordland's forest is largely determined by altitude. Lower elevations including the coastline are occupied by species tolerant of salt and exposure, such as mahoe (*Melicytus ramiflorus*) and pigeonwood (*Hedycarya arborea*). You do not have to travel far from the coast to more sheltered forests where the characteristic broadleaved species such as *Coprosma colensoi* come into their own. Other notables include lancewood (*Pseudopanax crassifolius*), mapou (*Myrsine australis*) and broadleaf (*Griselinia littoralis*). At higher altitudes there are species such as *Coprosma pseudocuneata*, mountain toatoa (*Phyllocladus aspleniifolius* var. *alpinus*) and near the treeline *Dracophyllum uniflorum*, *D. menziesii* and leatherwood (*Olearia colensoi*). Ground cover is mainly composed of mosses, astelias and ferns.

While tramping through the Fiordland forest, spare a thought for the forest floor, an often overlooked but equally remarkable part of the entire ecosystem. Without the fungi, bacteria and invertebrates that consume the litter, the recycling of nutrients would not take place.

The forests of Fiordland are among the least modified in New Zealand, thanks mostly to their isolation, but also to the protection afforded by national park status. Possums are the forest's greatest threat, munching through thousands of tonnes of rata, tree ferns and epiphytes every night. Red deer also favour succulent broadleaf trees and cause significant damage. The introduction of possum-control measures in valleys such as the Clinton and Arthur will undoubtedly enhance the forest's health.

THE ALPINE WORLD

The plants brave enough to venture above the treeline are rewarded with a stunning home, but have to cope with an environment that is harsh in the extreme. Take the Homer Tunnel area as an example, where avalanches are common, and violent winds, floods, landslips, droughts (relatively speaking) and tumbling boulders bring desolation to the landscape – but plants still survive. Other areas have high winds, extreme cold, snow coverage in winter, searing heat in summer, torrential rain and periodic disturbance of the soil.

Alpine plants have developed ingenious ploys to survive in their niches. Snow tussocks thwart the wind by weaving a dense mat of interlaced stems, trapping a layer of warm air near the ground. And they hibernate in winter, conserving moisture and nutrients. Other plants, such as celmisias, have a hairy felt on the leaf and stem known as a tomentum, the fine fuzz protecting them from the desiccating effect of wind. Some alpine plants, for example the Mount Cook lily, produce a type of anti-freeze using chemicals and salts in their retained moisture, which inhibits tissue damage from the expansion of freezing internal water. To keep grounded in moving scree slopes, many plants, including the coprosmas, send out snaking underground stems with tap roots that penetrate deeply into the soil like an anchor. During winter these perennials also die off, only to re-emerge the following spring and spread like a mat. This has the effect of binding the unconsolidated rocks, providing a seed bed for tussocks and other plants.

Of New Zealand's alpine plant species, 93 per cent are endemic to the New Zealand land mass, compared to 80 per cent of the vascular plants in general. And of the 24 plant species endemic to Fiordland, most are alpine. This high degree of endemism is usually associated with a long history of evolution in isolation, but it is generally agreed that alpine conditions have only been in existence in New Zealand for 2 million years. The most likely explanation is that the evolution has been rapid.

Another curious feature of the alpine flora is its split in distribution. For example, some plants are found only in Nelson and Fiordland and are absent from the intervening alpine regions. The best guess here is that during the last ice ages an ice sheet covered the entire central region, splitting the island with an uninhabitable zone under permanent snow and ice cover, and that the alpine plants have not yet reinvaded the gap.

Unlike their counterparts in Europe, New Zealand alpine flowers tend to come in muted colours such as white and yellow. A lack of specialised

IT RAINED AND RAINED

You may have heard that it rains a lot in Fiordland. There are a few reasons why.

Fiordland lies at the southern tip of New Zealand, in a belt of winds known as the Roaring Forties. These circumpolar winds oscillate below the subtropical high-pressure zone that is seemingly permanently anchored over Australia. The westerly winds are accentuated by the region's proximity to the Antarctic ice, which often dissipates a belt of cold air that causes a temperature gradient between it and Australia. This difference in temperatures is most marked in late spring, when it causes frequent equinoctial gales.

New Zealand is tucked away in its own corner of the South Pacific. Australia is 2000 km to the west, Antarctica 2500 km to the south. There is just ocean to the north, and Chile is 11,000 km away to the east. Any air mass on its way to New Zealand becomes so laden with moisture picked up from the ocean that it's ready to disgorge the pent-up vapour over the first bit of terra firma encountered. In the case of Fiordland, terra firma is high, very steep mountain sides that push the air up. As the air rises, it cools and the water vapour condenses into water droplets that amalgamate until they are heavy enough to form raindrops that fall back down to earth.

Meteorologists in Fiordland don't bother with millimetres and inches – rain is measured in metres. Te Anau, on the eastern side of the range, receives around 1.1 m per year. Puysegur Point on the south coast gets around 2 m per year. Doubtful Sound has over 5 m, below Milford Sound's average of 6.267 m per year.

Milford is one of the wettest places on earth at sea level. The highest recorded annual rainfall at Milford occurred in 1988, when the rain gauge tipped 9.2 m into the measuring tube. On 11 December that year, 521 mm fell in 24 hours. On the mountain tops, annual rainfall can exceed 15 m. Tropical showers seem like drizzle in this intensity, which can only be likened to someone emptying a bucket of water over your head.

Don't be put off – there is plenty of beauty associated with 'bad' weather. The high-intensity rainfall and the precipitous hillsides are the key ingredients for the legendary waterfalls that lace pollinating insects, such as long-tongued bees and butterflies, that are attracted to bright colours probably contributes to this.

As you walk up from the treeline, the alpine vegetation traverses several zones. The first is mixed snow tussock scrub with a variety of tall snow tussocks, shrubs and large herbs. The herbfields are characterised by taller daisy-like celmisias, buttercups and speargrass. On flatter ground, bogs are common in hollows and depressions, matted in a soft turf and mottled with small tarns. In the higher alpine zones, mostly above the domain of the Fiordland tramps, are fellfields and scree communities, where plants occupy scant soils or exploit moisture in crevices. Cushion plants such as rock sheep hug the ground and shelter from the wind.

the granite walls of the fiords. The forests also come alive when it is raining. The colours are vibrant, the smells fresh and the light uniform. When the world outside is masked by cloud, this is the time to look inwards to the domain of the trees. Rivers are roaring and sandflies are sheltering. Misty mountain tops appear during clear spells and sunbeams illuminate valley walls. The fiords are at their best during or after rain, when the land is seen in silhouette. Form rises over detail, shadow overrules light and mountain peaks float on a bed of cloud.

This anonymously written poem, apparently found in the Howden Hut book, tells the story.

It rained and rained and rained and rained
The average fall was well maintained
And when the tracks were simply bogs
It started raining cats and dogs.

After a drought of half an hour
We had a most refreshing shower
And then most curious thing of all
A steady rain began to fall.

Next day was also fairly dry
Save a deluge from the sky
Which wet the party to the skin
And then a gentle rain set in.

Remember, in Fiordland it only rains on around half of the days. But when it does rain, it does the job properly.

Identification of individual alpine species requires decades of study, but it's possible to learn the main groups with a curious mind and a little research. The main genera are as follows:

Buttercups: representatives in Fiordland include *Ranunculus lyallii* (Mount Cook lily, not actually a lily but the largest buttercup in the world) and *Ranunculus buchananii.*

Anisotome: a relative of the carrot family and with similar leaf forms.

Aciphylla: 40 alpine species distinguished by their sharp leaves, also known as speargrass or Spaniard. Fiordland representatives include *Aciphylla takahea, A. lyallii* and *A. congesta.*

Dracophyllum: prone to hybridise, the most commonly encountered are *D. menziesii* with its pineapple-like leaf head, *D. uniflorum* and *D. longifolium.*

Celmisia: one of the most important alpine genera with more than 50 representatives. Often called mountain daisies. Look for *C. ramulosa, C. bonplandii, C. petriei* and *C. traversii.*

Raoulia: cushion and mat plants sometimes with a spongy texture and a mosaic-like appearance.

Gentianella: the southern hemisphere version of the much loved European gentians, with similar delicate flowers.

Ourisia: only found in South America, Tasmania and New Zealand. Often found with white five-lobed leaves.

Hebe: nearly 100 New Zealand species, with opposite leaves and sometimes with a whipcord form.

Chionochloa: snow tussocks include *C. teretifolia* and *C. crassiuscula.* There are 22 species of snow tussock *Chionochloa* in Fiordland and all are endemic to New Zealand. *C. spiralis* is unique to the limestone regions near Lake Te Anau, seen on the Kepler, while *C. ovata* and *C. acicularis* are found only in Fiordland.

OUR FEATHERED FRIENDS

Before the arrival of humans, New Zealand was truly a land of birds. Having embarked on a voyage of evolutionary isolation for tens of millions of years, with only a few bats on board to represent the mammal class, birds ruled the kingdom. Sea birds in abundance nested on the coast and the forests were filled with the tuneful chorus of bird song.

The absence of ground predators fostered lines of avian genetics not encountered on other land masses. The plentiful supply of invertebrate life allowed an uncharacteristically high number of species, including the kiwi, kakapo and takahe, to lose the ability to fly. Why bother engineering light bones and strong wing muscles when the forest floor is a smorgasbord of insects, grubs and worms? Bird species tended to get very big, and evolved a sense of smell, whiskers and, in the case of kiwi, feathers that resemble fur. A curious trend emerged – in an ecological void, some birds were evolving into honorary mammals.

This avian paradise, where birds were free to roam without fear of predation, was abruptly shattered when the first Polynesians arrived, bringing with them kiore (Polynesian rats) and kuri (dogs). Able to negotiate branches, the rats devoured defenceless chicks. They scoffed eggs laid in tree hollows or scrapes in the ground. Many birds became extinct, including the Haast eagle and several species of the moa.

When the Europeans arrived vast tracts of forest habitat were cleared for pastures, and the introduction of the ship rat, Norway rat, cats, dogs, stoats, ferrets, weasels, possums, goats, deer and pigs heralded the demise of numerous species. The rats, cats and stoats were the main agents of extermination. Early European travellers in the Hollyford Valley might see a dead kakapo every 50 m after the first wave of stoats advanced down the valley. By the early 20th century the list of extinctions was long and many other species rested on the brink.

Avian good news stories do exist. In 1894, conservation in Fiordland began when Te Anau resident and passionate ornithologist Richard Henry was appointed caretaker of Resolution Island in an attempt to provide a haven for nurturing of endangered species. Half a century later the takahe, long thought extinct, was rediscovered in the Murchison Mountains. Today the Department of Conservation (DoC) is restoring areas such as the Eglinton, Clinton and Arthur Valleys with pest eradication and the reintroduction of species such as whio.

Other more resilient species have survived the onslaught. Some of the more likely encounters that will grace your tramps in the Fiordland forests may include the following birds.

> A visit to the Te Anau Wildlife Centre is a good introduction to the bird life of Fiordland and the opportunity to witness these species at close quarters. Information and some stuffed specimens are also on show at DoC's Fiordland National Park Visitor Centre.

Kaka *Nestor meridionalis*

You will normally hear the primeval screech of the kaka before sighting the distinctive scarlet under the olive-green wing. It is most likely to feed in the canopy, using its strong hooked beak to prise away bark and reveal the grubs lurking beneath. Morning and evening are the most common times to sight this member of the parrot family. A pleasing number live near the Divide at the start of the Routeburn Track and can show off with circus-like acts in the branches of the beech trees.

Kea *Nestor notabilis*

Resembling their cousin the kaka in appearance and with a distinctive 'keaaaaa' as their cry, kea are the mischievous mountain parrots that in one scientific study won the title of the world's most intelligent birds. They enjoy pastimes such as sliding down hut roofs at daybreak, prying rubber from windscreens and stealing unguarded lunches. Don't be tempted to feed them as they lose the ability to hunt and consequently starve in times when humans aren't around.

Tomtit *Petroica macrocephala* miromiro
Tomtits are easily distinguished by their black-and-white marking and diminutive stature. They are sociable birds, and attract your attention by flitting between branches.

Fantail *Rhipidura fuliginosa* piwakawaka
Fantails are the most endearing birds of Fiordland's forests. Performing a mesmerising acrobatic display in the foliage and chatting away with effervescent 'cheeps', these minuscule show-offs are hard to miss. On alighting, males especially fan their tails and drop their wings. The large tail feathers are used to execute abrupt changes of direction while hunting insects. When a fantail follows you through the forest, it is not being sociable, it is taking advantage of the insects you disturb in passing.

Bellbird *Anthornis melanura* korimako
With olive-green plumage, sleek figure and gently arcing beak, the bellbird is as attractive visually as its song is heavenly. The bell-like notes are learned from neighbouring adults and two birds may be heard in tandem, singing and counter-singing to determine territorial spacing. Members of the honeyeater family, bellbirds consume nectar from many native trees and in autumn, by feeding on berries, they act as important seed-dispersing agents in the ecology of the forest.

Tui *Prosthemadera novaeseelandiae*
Distinguished by aristocratic white throat tufts and possessing enviable skill in flight, tui are many forest visitors' favourite bird. They are most acclaimed for composing a symphonic repertoire of song that resonates through the forest canopy, filling the air with dulcet tones.

Like their musical colleagues the bellbirds, these honeyeaters feed on nectar and fruit, often travelling large distances to abundant food sources. Some New Zealand flowers such as the flax have co-evolved with the tui. The nectar treat is hidden about one tui beak length into the flower, so when the birds glean the sweet reward they powder their faces with the orange or yellow pollen from the stamens. This is then distributed to other flax flowers while the tui forage for their sugary fix.

Kereru *Hemiphaga novaeseelandiae* New Zealand pigeon
With its rich green back, white chest and oversize-pigeon form, the kereru is a conspicuous forest resident. It is often seen gorging on a variety of native fruits, such as coprosma berries, or resting on a sunny perch digesting its meal. Because of its wide gape, the kereru can eat large fruit. Little abrasion of the seed occurs in the gizzard, allowing seeds to pass through the digestive system intact. In this way the kereru ensures the perpetuation of its food source. Listen for the distinctive whistle of the kereru's wings as it negotiates obstacles on the flight path. On the tops, keep an eye out for lone birds travelling to faraway food sources.

Whio *Hymenolaimus malacorhynchos* blue duck
The whio, named by Maori for the sound of its call, lives by fast-flowing rivers in Fiordland's upper catchments. The handsome bird is often seen poised stoically on a boulder encircled by fast flowing water. The species is unique to New Zealand.
  Whio are fiercely territorial and will defend their patch aggressively, often fighting in pairs for their right to a waterway. They are picky with their water conditions, requiring bouldery streams in forest catchments, where the water is clear, the river banks are stable and there are plenty of invertebrates. Their presence is thus a good indicator of a catchment's health. Only around 700 pairs remain in the South Island.

Rifleman *Acanthisitta chloris* titipounamu
The tiny rifleman weighs in at a measly 6 g. The white eyebrow stripes and green/brown plumage are good camouflage in the dense forest, and it is only the birds' fluttering, skittish movements that give their presence away. Their cheeps are barely audible, but can often be heard as families work a habitual beat around their forest territories. The birds gained their European name from the fact their plumage resembles the uniform of an early colonial regiment.

New Zealand robin *Petroica australis* toutouwai
The endearing robins are among the forest's most gregarious birds. They seem to revel in human company, so long as you stay still or move only slowly. Once comfortable in your presence, they will often climb your legs or perch on boots to pick off sandflies at their leisure.

THE PEOPLE
AND THE LAND

MAORI IN FIORDLAND

According to one Maori legend, the fiords were carved by the demi-god Tu-te-Rakiwhanoa, who incised the unbroken mountain walls to create the indented coastline. His work started in the south, and like all new craftsmen, he started his project with gusto and enthusiasm. His skills, however, were not yet refined and his work was at times clumsy. The ragged coastline dotted with many islands is testimony to this inexperience. At one point the land on which his feet were anchored gave way, the ruptured rock splinters forming Secretary Island in Doubtful Sound and Resolution Island in Dusky Sound. As he worked north he developed into an accomplished craftsman and by the time he started on Milford Sound (Piopiotahi) his lines were clean, precise and dramatic. Piopiotahi is considered his masterpiece.

There are other traditions associated with Fiordland's landforms. It is said that the Te Anau and Manapouri Basins were carved out by Rakaihautu using his ko, or digging stick, and that the Takitimu Mountains are the result of the setting to stone of the Takitimu waka (canoe) commanded by Tamatea.

The main tribes in Fiordland were Ngati Mamoe, who arrived in the 16th century, and Ngai Tahu, who followed in the mid 17th century. From the late 18th century Ngati Mamoe, under chief Pukutahi, fled to Te Anau from Central Otago but many were chased and killed. Some retreated to the forests, giving rise to the myth of the Lost Tribe, although there is no evidence that they remained long in Fiordland's concealed valleys.

There is little sign of settlement on the coast south of Martins Bay, at the mouth of the Hollyford River, probably because of the extreme isolation and hostile conditions. Even today this stretch of coast is

POUNAMU   Pounamu, also called greenstone or New Zealand jade, has long been prized by Maori. Several myths relate to its formation and the tales of procurement of the 'stone of the gods' were shrouded in ritual. The stone is found only in the South Island and thus is very significant to Ngai Tahu.

Nephrite jade, the hard form found west and north of Lake Wakatipu, was used to make tools, weaponry and ornaments. Pounamu chisels and adzes were used for tree felling, hollowing out logs for waka (canoes), and in buildings and their associated elaborate carvings. The stone was also used to make mere or patu pounamu, a club-like weapon. Ornaments included hei-tiki, a neck pendant in the stylised form of a human, replicas of which are now peddled in tourists shops all over the country.

Anita Bay, at the mouth of Milford Sound, was the only source anywhere in New Zealand for a slightly soft form of pounamu known as tangiwai (tears from weeping). The name recalls the sorrowful journey of Tama-ki-te-rangi in search of his estranged wives. He found one of them near Milford Sound but she had been turned to stone. Tama's tears penetrated the rock, metamorphising to translucent tangiwai.

This form of the precious stone, also known as bowenite, could be formed into implements with high cutting angles, such as chisels and gouges. Its translucent appearance, however, gave it great value in jewellery making and tangiwai was esteemed by chiefs of high mana.

Early Maori travelling between Anita Bay and Central Otago with pounamu followed a route either along today's Milford Track, or up the Hollyford Valley to the Greenstone Valley. Wearing only roughly woven sandals, these hardy folk lived off the land, eating eels, fish and forest birds. Routes were described in song and in this way mental maps, including places of shelter, food and obstacles, were passed through generations.

uninhabited, so it comes as no surprise Maori found other more suitable sites.

Radiocarbon dating of archaeological finds suggests a Maori presence in Takahe Valley, near Te Anau, from the 17th century, but these settlements were, like most others in the region, seasonal. Other evidence from coastal caves and middens includes fireplaces, fishing lines, wooden floats, fish-bone hooks and flax rope. At some sites at the northern end of Lake Te Anau drying racks, used for food preservation, have been discovered. Most archaeological evidence of Maori occupation in Fiordland is confined to caves.

Dwellings were generally small huts or rock shelters, although some buildings were a conical structure of interlaced sticks thatched with flax. Fireplaces were open and kept deliberately smoky to deter sandflies. Other means in the armoury against the marauding bloodsuckers were rather less delectable – to smother the skin in mud or pungent seal fat.

Clothing consisted of a kakahu, a woven flax cloak, often decorated with feathers or dog skin. This was worn over a maro or rapaki, a short kilt. A pake was the equivalent of our Gore-Tex jacket, a rain cape fashioned from tightly woven flax, kiekie leaves or sheets of totara bark. Paraerae or sandals were similarly woven from flax or cabbage tree leaves. In the high country a soft matting of dried grass provided a modicum of insulation from the cold ground.

Seals and birds, including moa from the Te Anau Basin, were staples of the diet. By the 18th century, with the extinction of the moa, birds such as kakapo, kiwi, takahe, weka, kereru and kaka were also on the menu. Kaimoana, the bountiful resources of the sea, did not go unnoticed, with estuarine fish including flounder and whitebait harvested from Martins Bay. The main vegetable eaten was the ubiquitous aruhe (fern root).

Travel was difficult in the treacherous seas, where only downwind travel was really possible. Sea-going vessels were commonly fashioned from totara and made double-hulled to give extra stability. Single-hulled waka (canoes) were used on the lakes and on the Waiau River.

In drier eastern areas, Maori lit fires to clear the forest. Grass, fern and shrubs colonised the bare ground, and significant regeneration was inhibited by further fires. One theory suggests these fires were lit to encourage the growth of bracken fern, which took advantage of the burnt deep soils, fertilised by the forest ash.

In the harsh climes of Fiordland, early Ngai Tahu became familiar with the slower pace of nature, the differences in flora and fauna and the abundance of sea mammals. Most of these resources were managed by a complex social structure relying on the administration by whanau (families) and hapu (wider families). The most prominent members were known as kaitiaki or guardians. Nature was revered and its doings were inextricably linked to human fortunes and rhythms.

The arrival of the Europeans changed everything. Throughout New Zealand the Maori population succumbed to European diseases, and following the Treaty of Waitangi in 1840, most of the original tribal lands were misappropriated and Maori were left landless and rootless. Land in the Greenstone, Caples, Rees, Dart and Routeburn Valleys was cut and burnt by Europeans in preparation for pastoral activities.

In 1998, an act of Parliament allotted compensation for these wrongdoings to Ngai Tahu and the earlier tribal groupings of Waitaha and Ngati Mamoe that come under its banner. It confirmed Ngai Tahu's right to express its traditional kaitiaki relationship with the environment. Tribal redress, an apology from the Crown, and acknowledgement of the role of taonga Aoraki (the tribe's treasures) were also included. Economic redress in the form of a payment of $170 million plus the ability to purchase property from the Crown enabled the iwi to set up a self-governing system of resource allocation.

Ngai Tahu has established itself as an economic powerhouse within the South Island, with an investment portfolio including interests in fishing, tourism and property, as well as a diversified equities portfolio. Some profits from the business ventures are allocated to deliver social benefits back to the people of the iwi. More than 20,000 people of Ngai Tahu descent have reforged links with their tribal lands and are once again in touch with how their ancestors would have interacted with the landscapes of the region. They hold mana whenua in the southern land.

EUROPEANS IN FIORDLAND

For a place so impenetrable, remote and rugged, Fiordland has seen an extraordinary concentration of human endeavour since the arrival of the first European explorers.

James Cook arrived in 1770 on his first voyage to New Zealand and passed the Fiordland coast but did not venture into the fiords. Three years later on his second visit, having jostled with icebergs in the Southern Ocean and in need of rest and sustenance, he took *Resolution* into Dusky Sound. The five-week stay proved to be one of Cook's most productive and scientifically rewarding sojourns in New Zealand.

Extensive repairs were carried out on *Resolution* and the holds were restocked with fish, fowl and seals. The crew experimented with brewing beer from rimu and tea from manuka. Botanists J. R. Forster and A. E. Sparrman conducted extensive surveys of the flora. Cook took a longboat from the ship and charted the sound with details embellished by William Hodges' sketchbook. William Wales set up an observatory on Astronomers Point, the headland next to Pickersgill Harbour where *Resolution* was moored, and chance meetings with local Maori families gave Cook an insight into their customs and culture.

In 1791 George Vancouver, who had been aboard *Resolution*, returned with *Discovery* and *Chatham* and spent three weeks exploring Breaksea and Dusky Sounds. Two years later an Italian captain, Alessandro Malaspina, commanded a Spanish mission in Doubtful Sound. They stayed just a night, but left the only Spanish names on the New Zealand map.

These early visitors noted the abundance of fur seals on the coastal rocks, prompting interest from sealers. In 1792 William Raven left a sealing gang in Dusky Sound. Under the command of William Leith, 12 men settled in at Luncheon Cove, built houses and a 16 m boat and during their stay of a little over 10 months amassed 4500 seal skins. From the 1820s the wholesale slaughter of the pinnipeds continued, mainly to supply the Chinese market. The tallies for skins exported make for appalling reading and include figures such as 60,000 skins leaving aboard the *Favorite*.

Whalers were next, spurred by disappointing results from Australian waters and by the frequent sightings by sealers of whales off the Fiordland coast and in Foveaux Strait. In 1799 the whaler *Britannia* left the New Zealand fishery with more than 23,875 litres of sperm whale oil. In 1829 Peter Williams bought land at Preservation Inlet from chief Taboca and established the Cuttle Cove whaling station. Over a period of eight years, exports averaged more than 145,000 litres per year of whale oil.

Captain John Grono aboard the *Elizabeth* was the first European to enter Milford Sound some time between 1809 and 1821, the entrance having been missed by previous explorers on account of its being concealed. It was not until 1851, however, that a comprehensive survey was undertaken by Captain John Lort Stokes of HMS *Acheron*. The painstaking attention to detail by the crew made it the most complete survey available for more than 100 years.

In the same year, C. J. Nairn and W. H. Stephen left Riverton with Maori guides and made a week-long journey up the Waiau River to Te Anau. They were the first Europeans to venture this far inland in Fiordland. It was not until 1863 that the first European east–west crossing of Otago was completed, by Patrick Quirk Caples (see panel). In 1870 a new port at Martins Bay, called Jamestown, was settled. By 1879, with the shipping service discontinued because the bar was unnavigable and no hope of a road to Queenstown being completed, the town had been abandoned.

In 1885 the keeper of Puysegur lighthouse, Philip Payn, discovered gold on Coal Island, at the mouth of Preservation Inlet. News got out, even from this most isolated outpost, and by 1890 there were avid

A ROUTE TO THE COAST

During the 1860s gold rushes of Central Otago, the gold found had to be taken to the nearest bank – in Melbourne. The precious metal had to be loaded onto packhorses and transported to Dunedin, from where a ship took it through the treacherous waters of Foveaux Strait and over the Tasman to Australia. The risk of losing a boat was high, so investors were keen to establish a port on the west coast. Then there would be only the Tasman to worry about.

With this in mind, government gold prospector Patrick Quirk Caples travelled up the Route Burn from the Dart Valley, at the head of Lake Wakatipu, in 1863. He discovered a lake 'surrounded by glacier covered pinnacles' at the head of the valley, which he named Lake Harris after John Hyde Harris, the superintendent of Otago. Although it was January, Caples had to use his shovel to make steps in the snow bordering the lake. After crossing Harris Saddle, he dropped down to the fast-flowing Hollyford River, which he named after his birthplace in County Tipperary, Ireland. He followed the river downstream as far as Hidden Falls Creek.

With food resources dwindling, Caples was forced to retreat to the Route Burn. Once he had restocked he returned to Harris Saddle and, encountering clear skies, was able to see down the Hollyford Valley all the way to the coast at Martins Bay. He could make out a sizeable lake before the coast, which he called Lake McKerrow after surveyor James McKerrow, who was also exploring the region at the time. He also spied a plume of smoke rising from the beach. Not having enough supplies to make it to the coast, Caples descended from the saddle and returned to Lake Wakatipu via the Caples Valley.

On his next foray, Caples ascended the Greenstone Valley then followed the Hollyford, skirting fossickers on the mainland nearby. James Smith was the first to strike it lucky and the town of Cromarty soon sprung up, including the usual necessities such as a school, post office, sawmill and hotels. More gold was found nearby at Te Oneroa and the Morning Star battery constructed to process the ore.

Settlement of inland areas of Fiordland ran in parallel with coastal development. Freeman Jackson built a house at Balloon Loop, just south of Te Anau, in the early 1850s. He was followed in 1858 by Donald Hankinson and in 1860 by John and Henry Hodge, who established Te Anau Downs station.

The tourism potential of Milford Sound was apparent early on, and Quintin McKinnon's discovery of an overland route via the Clinton and Arthur Valleys in 1888 got things going. The following year, William Henry Homer scaled the saddle that now bears his name and identified the route of the present Milford Road. From the early 1900s well-heeled tourists were voyaging to Glade House at the head of Lake Te Anau

the shore of Lake McKerrow, to the coast. At Martins Bay he found the 'rudely constructed' huts of a Maori camp, which he presumed was peopled with cannibals. He hid his presence from the Maori, writing in his diary, 'It is easy for a person to find courage when he has law and assistance at his back, but let him be alone and beyond any assistance, near the camp of savages, and he will find how fleeting courage is.'

In his search for gold Patrick Quirk Caples failed, but in the first European east–west crossing of Otago he succeeded. During his explorations he established the basis for today's Routeburn, Caples, Greenstone and Hollyford Tracks.

Next on the scene was James Hector, provincial geologist for Otago. In August 1863, Hector landed at Martins Bay from the schooner *Matilda Hayes*. Caples's fears were unfounded – Hector was met and entertained by chief Tutoko, with whom he struck up a lasting friendship. He returned to Queenstown by travelling up the Hollyford Valley and Pass Creek, and down the Greenstone Valley to Lake Wakatipu. This route, he declared, would be perfect for a road.

The proposal was taken up by the superintendent of Otago, James Macandrew, who had grand plans for a port on the west coast to be called Jamestown. But instead of following Hector's recommendation, surveyor James McKerrow supported taking the road up the Route Burn and over Harris Saddle. He reckoned it would take a day to walk the roughly 90 km from Lake Wakatipu to the Hollyford Valley and, despite the fact Caples had found snow on the saddle in January, surmised it would be impassable for only a few weeks each winter. He grossly underestimated the challenges and costs of the project and after four years work ceased.

before embarking on the Milford Track, which would soon be dubbed 'the finest walk in the world'. Construction on the Milford Road began in the early 1930s, although it wasn't until 1954, when the Homer Tunnel opened, that this transport corridor into the heart of Fiordland allowed tourism en masse.

The southern reaches of Fiordland around Waitutu caught the eye of loggers and grand plans were hatched to establish a sawmill at Port Craig. The 'think big' ideology of the day failed in this case, but not before a reckless attitude to the cheque book allowed some impressive infrastructural development, including viaducts for a tramline. The Tuatapere Hump Ridge Track explores the legacy of this milling operation.

To the earliest human visitors, both Maori and European, Fiordland was a wild and forbidding place, remote and challenging to inhabit. As you walk through the unspoiled mountains and valleys today, you cannot help but be in awe of those early folk who explored one of Earth's finest landscapes.

HUTS 'N' STUFF

The following sections are provided to introduce the 'nuts and bolts' of tramping in Fiordland, all those logistical details that need taking care of before you venture into the hills. This includes notes on track accommodation, what to put in your pack and what to wear, and how to stay safe.

TRACK ACCOMMODATION

Tramping huts have been a feature in Fiordland for over a century, since Quintin McKinnon erected his first rather rudimentary structures on the Milford Track. The busiest DoC huts have been staffed by rangers since 1968. The buildings themselves have come a long way from the crude unlined huts of yesteryear and the Great Walks huts now boast flushing toilets, gas cookers, solar panels and mattresses.

At busy times of year huts can be filled to overcapacity, which is why the Great Walks system was introduced. The arrangements vary from track to track, but on the Milford, Routeburn and Kepler walks all huts and campsites must be booked in advance for the peak season from the end of October to the end of April. Outside the season, the facilities revert to 'back-country' status just the same as all other walks. This means beds are available on a first-come first-served basis.

The Great Walks can be booked online at the DoC website or by contacting a DoC visitor centre. For all other tracks you either need to pre-purchase hut tickets (each hut is usually two tickets or $10 per night) or buy an annual pass ($90) that allows unlimited nights in all huts except those on the Great Walks.

Christmas/New Year and Easter are very busy and around these times you'd be wise to carry a tent on trips with unbooked huts (Hollyford, Greenstone and Caples, and Rees–Dart) to avoid the unfortunate scenario of arriving at a hut in the dark and pelting rain, tired and hungry and with no sense of humour, to find all the beds are occupied.

Camping is permitted on all the tracks in this book except the Milford and Hump Ridge. Campers are not allowed to use hut facilities on the Great Walks. Campsites on Great Walks must also be booked in advance.

Hut living is not conducive to sleep. Canvas-covered mattresses, sleeping bags that rustle, plastic bags that crackle, snorers, farters, people getting up early or arriving late, echoey wooden construction – all these make for a poor night's sleep, despite the physical exertions. For some this is not an issue, but if it sounds bothersome try earplugs or whisky.

On the Kepler, Milford and Routeburn Great Walks, full-time rangers live at the huts during the peak season. The other tracks in this book have wardens in the huts during summer, although they may rotate between huts. It's a common misconception that rangers spend all day sitting around admiring the majestic scenery. This is very far from the truth. Although they are fortunate to have the New Zealand back country as their office, there are real responsibilities. Rangers are usually storehouses of useful information for trampers. They maintain the tracks – this can involve clearing the water tables, building up the tracks and cutting back ferns. The commute can sometimes be a few hours' walk (and, for the record, most rangers walk in with eight days' worth of food on their

DOC VISITOR CENTRES

Fiordland National Park
Visitor Centre
Lakefront Drive
Te Anau 9600
0-3-249 7924
fiordlandvc@doc.govt.nz

Queenstown Visitor Centre
Shotover Street
Queenstown 9300
0-3-442 7935
queenstownvc@doc.govt.nz

Glenorchy Visitor Centre
Closed in 2007

For opening times and
further information visit
www.doc.govt.nz

backs). And from time to time their work is a matter of life and death, as injuries are common and medical emergencies arise.

To keep yourself safe and your impact small in the huts:

- Leave huts as you would like to find them.
- Take care with fires and never leave them unattended.
- Pack it in, pack it out. You brought your food with you, so carry out the rubbish. Even better, pick up the muesli bar wrappers and apple stickers you often see on the tracks.

DEPARTMENT OF CONSERVATION

In New Zealand all our conservation land, accounting for nearly 30 per cent of the country's total land area, is administered by the Department of Conservation (DoC). All conservation land is also public land, and there is a high level of public input into conservation management.

DoC's responsibility and mission is 'to conserve New Zealand's natural and historic heritage for all to enjoy now and in the future'. The department's responsibilities are summarised in its Maori name, Te Papa Atawhai. 'Te papa' refers to a box or container (for treasures) and 'atawhai' the act of nurturing or preserving.

The guiding document of Te Papa Atawhai is the 1987 Conservation Act, which sets out a difficult task for the department to perform, including the management of land and other natural and historic resources, preserving freshwater and recreational fisheries, advocating and promoting the benefits of conservation and fostering recreation opportunities. To this end, DoC administers the country's 14 national parks, with more than 12,500 km of walking and tramping tracks, around 1000 back-country huts and more than 10,000 structures. It also manages conservation areas, scenic reserves, historic reserves and marine reserves.

SOME THOUGHTS ON GEAR

Your local outdoor retailer, friends with tramping experience and other outdoor books can give guidance on exactly what you need to take with you on a multi-day tramp, but here are a few ideas based on personal experience. It is not a comprehensive list of items to pack.

The most important thing to remember is to pack light. I don't mind being grotty while tramping – I'd much prefer to wear the same T-shirt for the entire tramp than carry clean (and dirty) ones for the whole trip. Remember also that you are venturing into a dynamic environment, where all the elements can be thrown at you in a single day. Good gear can be a life-saver, so don't skimp. If you don't want to buy, then hire. Try also to pack intelligently. Put the stuff you need most often at the top or in an outer pocket of your pack. Keep items you'll need at the same time (e.g. wet-weather gear, dry clothing or lunch food) in bags together.

Equipment can be bought or hired in Te Anau and Queenstown.

SANDFLIES Much has been said of that diminutive sandfly. Captain Cook had his problems with them. In 1773 he described them as 'The most mischievous animals here. . .very numerous and so troublesome that they exceed everything of the kind I ever met with. Wherever they bite they cause a swelling, and such an intolerable itching that it is not possible to refrain from scratching, which at last brings on ulcers like the small-pox.' He was a well-travelled fellow, so these are damning words indeed. Austrian naturalist and taxidermist Andreas Reischek couldn't tolerate them when he visited Fiordland in the 1880s. 'I was so pestered with sandflies, I was frequently compelled to run away from them and bathe my eyes.' But the most common epithet flung around is 'annoying little bastards'. The sorry fact is that you must put up with sandflies or go home.

According to Maori legend the sandflies were put here by Hine-nui-te-po, the goddess of death. She was so impressed with the handiwork of Tu-te-Rakiwhanoa, the master carver of Fiordland, that she worried others would linger too long and become entranced by the landscape. She released one large sandfly and many small ones and their descendants now ensure that you keep moving.

Sandflies mainly feed on the blood of lizards, beetles, seals, bats and introduced mammals. Males live off the sap of plants and have not educated females that blood sucking is a harder means of procuring nourishment. The sandfly life cycle involves the laying of rafts of eggs under the surface of a stream. Eggs anchor themselves from the posterior end with a sucker on hooked gelatinous threads, which also strain food from the water. When the egg needs to move, new threads are thrown out and the insect loops-the-loop and leapfrogs downstream. Eventually the cone-shaped pupa attaches itself to a rock. The seven-week cycle is completed when the dastardly sandfly rises to the surface in a bubble.

Free to roam, the female sandfly pursues her blood-pumping prey with gusto and determination. When she bites, an anti-coagulant is released to stop the proboscis from blocking. It is this anti-coagulant that causes the unsightly swelling and downright annoying itch.

Te Anau retailers include Outside Sports, which is open seven days a week in summer 9 am to 9 pm (www.teanausports.co.nz). It also has a big hire department. Bev's Tramping Gear Hire (www.bevs-hire.co.nz) is an efficient Te Anau outfit with a Great Walks special that includes pack, pack liner, sleeping bag, parka, overtrousers, fleece jacket, micro-fleece, polypropylene top and longs, hat, mittens, cooking pans, bowls, cup, cutlery, torch, guidebooks, maps and walking pole. It does not include boots or food. Bookings are essential from November to March. The best known Queenstown retailer is also Outside Sports (www.outsidesports.co.nz) – it has a hire department too – but there are any number of outdoors shops to choose from.

There are a few sandfly myths out there.

- *Myth 1: Sandflies have trouble flying in winds greater than 8 km/h.* This is wholly untrue – even in strong winds they can manage neat landings on bare skin.
- *Myth 2: Sandflies won't get you if it's raining.* It may be true that sandflies can't fly in the rain, but as soon as you get to shelter you'll find that's where they are all hiding.
- *Myth 3: Sandflies can't bite through clothing.* It's true they can't bite through heavy clothing, but polyprop is no barrier to the sandfly proboscis.
- *Myth 4: As long as you are moving, the sandflies won't bite.* Actually this one is true, but the problem is you are going to want to stop occasionally to admire the view or rest or eat or talk or write or photograph, and they'll be waiting.

There's always insect repellent. The most effective ones contain DEET (N,N-diethyl-m-toluamide), a powerful chemical developed by the US Army after World War II for use in jungle warfare. There have been claims that it poses risks to human health, but studies have not shown it does significant harm when used in an approved way. Some brands of insect repellent contain as much as 70 per cent DEET, which is strong enough to make dye run. One tramper I met had half his face go temporarily numb smearing this concentration on.

If you want to steer clear of DEET, permethrin-based repellents have also been shown to work. Some people say a mixture of baby oil, sun cream and citronella works well, while others swear by a 50–50 mix of Dettol and baby oil. My experience is that all brands and recipes will reduce bites by around 70 per cent, but you are still going to get bitten. The only sure-fire way to remain bite-free is to tramp in a neoprene wetsuit with a balaclava, mask and snorkel.

Don't let the bastards get you down. And remember, if you don't scratch, it won't itch so much.

Boots

These are the most important piece of tramping equipment. Boots are your friends – treat them well and they in turn will look after you. I prefer boots with leather uppers, as these can be taken home, cleaned, dried slowly and waterproofed to be as good as new for the next trip. I wear one pair of thick socks.

If your boots are new, wear them in well before your big trip. The Fiordland tops in inclement weather is not the place to find out your boots are uncomfortable or give you blisters. Do some practice walks, including up hills, in your chosen boot and sock combination.

Pack

The next most important bit of kit is your pack. Don't go too big – 55 litres is ample for most people. The larger your pack, the more unneeded items you will fill it with. Pack light and you will significantly enhance your enjoyment. Your pack should have an adjustable waist strap and harness system independent of the body of the pack. Adjust the harness so that as much of the weight as possible is on your waist and the pack isn't pulling back on your shoulders, inhibiting circulation to your arms.

Pack all your gear into a pack liner. Cheap bin bags don't do the job, you need heavy plastic. Don't rely on one of those external shower covers – they are useless in Fiordland rain.

Clothing

You must take a jacket that will keep out wind and rain or you're on a certain road to hypothermia. But don't expect to stay perfectly dry – good waterproof fabrics, even Gore-Tex, may not be able to keep out the best Fiordland can throw at you. Whatever fabric you choose it should be breathable, otherwise the inside will get as wet as the outside.

Merino wool tops are a great invention. I have one thin layer of merino next to the skin, a midweight and a top layer plus a spare thin layer for wearing at night in the hut. You can't beat the Icebreaker brand. Even though their garments are pricey, they are the best and still look smart enough to wear to a swanky city bar after 150 days' wear.

You'll need a warm beanie, gloves and a sunhat. For the hut you might like a spare dry beanie as well as spare warm socks and hut shoes to walk from the communal areas to the bunk rooms. 'Crocs and socks' seems to be the latest bush fashion.

It's good to have two pairs of polypropylene leggings: one for walking in if it's cold and another dry set for hut wear. Kiwi trampers normally wear shorts over the top of the leggings. Waterproof overtrousers are a good idea, but make sure you can get them on and off easily without taking your boots off. Gaiters keep the grit out of your boots, allow you to cross knee-deep streams without getting wet feet and ward off the sandflies from your lower legs.

Food

Keep it light and dehydrated – plenty of snacks with lots of energy. Couscous is quick and easy to prepare and is fuel efficient. You never enjoy food more than when you are in the hills, so don't discount taking fresh vegetables. They are light, easy to cook and are the envy of those picking at dehydrated peas. Carrots, cauliflower, courgette, and green beans stay reasonably fresh over two to three days.

On non-Great Walks you will need your own stove and utensils. Even on Great Walks a warm drink in a shelter can be a lifesaver when it's raining horizontally outside.

Other stuff

A torch is essential. How did people survive before headlamps? Pocket knives should be kept light. Buy a decent water bottle as the plastic ones can alter form and break with variations in altitude. Visit www.mountainsafety.org.nz for links to first-aid kit retailers. For expensive camera gear, dry bags are an added insurance. They are stocked in all outdoor shops.

SAFETY AND SECURITY

Fiordland is one of the most dynamic landscapes on the planet. When you tramp in there, your safety is your responsibility. There may be hut wardens who will organise help if you don't turn up on a Great Walk, there may·be mountain radios, intentions forms and Search and Rescue

NEW ZEALAND ENVIRONMENTAL CARE CODE

1. Protect rare and endangered plants and animals.
2. Remove rubbish. Take it away with you.
3. Bury toilet waste in a shallow hole away from waterways, tracks, campsites and huts.
4. Keep streams clean.
5. Take care with fires. If you must build a fire, keep it small, use dead wood, and douse it with water when you leave. Before you go, remove any evidence. Portable stoves are preferable, as they are more efficient and pose less risk to the environment.
6. After camping, leave the site as you found it.
7. Keep to the track. This minimises the chances of treading on fragile seedlings.
8. Respect the cultural heritage.
9. Enjoy yourself.
10. Consider others. Respect everybody's reasons for wanting to enjoy the region's beauty.

helicopters, but ultimately these should only be used as last resorts. Far too often trampers are evacuated by helicopter from the Fiordland tracks not because they have suffered an accident beyond all reasonable control, but because they have made poor decisions with the information available.

Going tramping in Fiordland is strenuous physical exercise. You will be on uneven surfaces, climbing over 1000 vertical metres or more, carrying heavy loads and battling the elements. It's OK to challenge yourself, but if you are not fit enough, you are more likely to lose concentration, fall, and sprain or break a limb. If you are not fit enough for the walk you are undertaking, you risk your safety and the safety of those who have to come and get you if you have an accident.

Check the weather. If severe gales or snow are predicted, change your plans. Too many people head out on the Fiordland tracks in bad conditions, thinking they'll never have another opportunity. They have planned a tramp as a highlight of their New Zealand or South Island trip and are damn well going to do it. But the tracks will always be here. You might have to come back another time, but at least you'll be alive to do so. All DoC centres have weather forecasts with weather warnings. Heed them. The DoC website (www.doc.govt.nz) has links to good forecasts and if you know how to read weather maps, you can't beat the forecast charts on www.metvuw.com.

Get the right gear. Take a first-aid kit. On DoC Great Walks and the

Hump Ridge Track, the hut wardens will generally know numbers and be able to raise the alarm if you don't show up, but if you are doing a non-Great Walks trip, fill out an intentions form at the local DoC centre, or tell a friend or relative when you expect to return. Remember to tell DoC or the friend or relative when you have returned. Don't let Search and Rescue and the police risk their lives looking for you in the hills while you are sitting in a warm pub somewhere.

Pick your season. The only tramps featured in this book that are possible over winter are the Hump Ridge, Hollyford, and Greenstone and Caples Tracks (although crossing McKellar Saddle may present problems after snow). The Hollyford is valley floor all the way and stays milder than the eastern side of the ranges. Attempting any other track in winter is virtual suicide as they cross numerous avalanche paths. Even with extensive mountain experience, the right gear and a good understanding of snowpack stability, the risks are still high.

Before the winter's first snowfall can be a good time to beat the crowds and benefit from clear autumn light. If you're contemplating walking any time out of the main walking season, contact DoC first – and heed their advice.

Keep to the track and take a map. The best ones by far are the recreational maps produced by Terralink. They are the standard 1:50,000 topographical maps with other features of note superimposed. The maps available for the Fiordland walks are Milford & Kepler Tracks, Greenstone & Routeburn Tracks, Aspiring & Rees–Dart Recreation Areas. For the other tracks use the NZ260 1:50,000 series.

It is recommended you take a personal locator beacon with you, especially if travelling out of season. These can be activated in an emergency and emit a radio signal that can be picked up by Search and Rescue and your position identified, drastically reducing the time it takes for them to find you. These can be hired from Mobil Te Anau (0-3-249 7247), with the cost subsidised by a charitable trust. They may also be available for hire in Queenstown, Glenorchy and Tuatapere – ask at the visitor centre.

Take care with your drinking water. There is some debate about the potability of Fiordland water. DoC advises you to boil all water for 3 minutes to eliminate the chance of your getting giardia, a water-borne intestinal parasite. But if you only take water from flowing watercourses that have not drained through farmland, you will likely be safe. I drink water from rivers and lakes and so do my kids. This doesn't mean that you are 100 per cent safe, however, so if in doubt, heed DoC advice.

There is a small risk of vehicles being broken into, but in Te Anau safer parking can be organised by phoning 0-3-249 7198 or 025 260 9032 or email saferparkingteanau@msn.com. You will find their website at www.saferparking.co.nz. Many people park their vehicles by the DoC centre in Te Anau. In Tuatapere, private vehicles can be left at the Hump Ridge Track office or Rarakau car park ($5 per vehicle donation is appreciated). All vehicles are left at the owner's risk.

Most accommodation providers in Te Anau and Queenstown will store your gear while you're in the hills. Even if you are not staying there, for a fee you can leave gear or a vehicle at Te Anau Lakeview Holiday Park (0-3-249 7457). Info & Track, 37 Shotover Street, Queenstown (0-3-442 9708) also offers gear storage.

TUATAPERE
HUMP RIDGE TRACK

60 km ■ three days ■ loop

The Tuatapere Hump Ridge Track is a gem, presently less frequented than such showy tramps as the Milford, Routeburn and Kepler Tracks. Given time and publicity, however, it will surely become renowned as a classic tramp. The track venture is a community initiative developed after the Forest Service stopped operating in Tuatapere in 1984. It makes use of the Hump Ridge nearby and provides a quality tramping experience. Numbers are set to build from the 2500 annually at present.

The tramp starts with a leg-stretching jaunt along Bluecliffs Beach before a challenging climb through beech forest to an alpine landscape made eerie by convoluted columns of weathered sandstone that rise like sentinels above the tarns. Okaka Hut is the first night's stop. On day two the snaking boardwalks descend between alpine bogs, tors and gnarled goblin forest. Intermittent lookouts spoil for choice – gaze east over Te Waewae Bay and the Waiau Valley, west into the vast expanse of Fiordland or to the Southern Ocean. On reaching the terrace above the coastline, you will rejoin the South Coast Track. This former tramline route once serviced the Port Craig mill, crossing viaducts including the one over the Percy Burn. At Port Craig you can descend to the beach or lookout to see if the Hector's dolphins are around. Day three is mostly a day of beaches. The track undulates between bays, from the shade of the cool forest to the golden sands. It then rejoins the track along Bluecliffs Beach.

The historic mill at Port Craig is not the only link to timber – it was the much more recent closure of sawmills in the Tuatapere area that led to the development of the Hump Ridge Track as a means of providing employment. The Tuatapere Hump Track Charitable Trust was entrusted with the task of planning and construction.

It hasn't been an easy ride for the trust. It raised funds totalling more than $3 million, but red tape around access – the track crosses both

SECTION TIMINGS

DAY ONE   8 hours 21 km

Rarakau to Track Burn	1¾ hours	6 km
Track Burn to Flat Creek	45 min	2 km
Flat Creek to third bridge	1¾ hours	4 km
Third bridge to Stag Point	2¼ hours	4 km
Stag Point to Okaka Hut	45 min	3 km
Summit walk (optional)	45 min	3 km return

DAY TWO   8 hours 21 km

Okaka Hut to Luncheon Rock	2¼ hours	6 km
Luncheon Rock to Edwin Burn viaduct	2½ hours	5 km
Edwin Burn viaduct to Peter Burn viaduct	20 min	1.5 km
Peter Burn viaduct to Port Craig	2 hours	6.5 km
Port Craig Heritage Trail (optional)	45 min	2 km return

DAY THREE   6 hours 18 km

Port Craig to Blowhole Beach	2½ hours	8 km
Blowhole Beach to Flat Creek	45 min	2 km
Flat Creek to Rarakau	2½ hours	8 km

conservation and private land – entangled and frustrated the trustees. It took around a decade before the track was ready to be opened by Prime Minister Helen Clark on 1 November 2001.

When the Hump Ridge Track first opened, it gained a reputation for being muddy. The quagmire has, however, been overcome with the construction of significant sections of boardwalk that protect the fragile environment and save boots, gaiters and knees from mud. When I walked the track there had been three good storms in the previous three weeks, the last being five days before. The mud was rarely deeper than my boots. But don't imagine this is some sanitised form of tramping. Your boots will need some TLC in a few days. You should also be aware this is quite a tough tramp, with three big days. You will earn that hot bath the day after tomorrow!

BOOKING

The Tuatapere Hump Ridge Track is a private venture and you must book your accommodation before departure. In the summer season the track office is open seven days a week from 8.30 am to 5.30 pm, with longer hours (7.30 am to 7.30 pm) in peak season. In winter it is open Wednesday to Sunday 10.30 am to 3.30 pm but email and phone messages are checked daily.

Tuatapere Hump Ridge Track
Tuatapere Information Centre
31 Orawia Road
Tuatapere
Southland 9620

0-3-226 6739
Freephone (NZ only)
0800 HUMP RIDGE (0800 486 774)

contact@humpridgetrack.co.nz
www.humpridgetrack.co.nz

There are various options for the level of luxury you indulge in, including having your gear choppered to the huts, as well as a fully guided option. The 40-bunk huts are as well-stocked as a posh motel unit, complete with coffee plungers, quiche dishes and pillows. The seats are padded and there are libraries, and interesting characters enliven the evening chatter. Okaka is superbly sited on the ridge with endless views over the south coast, while Port Craig is right on the coast.

Camping is permitted only at Port Craig, near the DoC hut.

There is a map of the track on the website, and the NZ260 series map C46 Port Craig covers the area of the walk, although older printings do not have the track marked. An alternative is to download TUMONZ, software with the complete 1:50,000 series, from www.tumonz.co.nz.

GETTING THERE

From Tuatapere follow signs along SH 99 to the junction with Papatotara Road then onto Papatotara Coast Road. The final 7 km is gravel road, including a stretch along the beach that can be affected by storms and high spring tides. The road passes the signposted start to the track just before the Rarakau car park, at the end of the public road, where vehicles may safely be left ($5 donation per vehicle). Alternatively you can leave your vehicle at the Tuatapere Hump Ridge Track office and take track transport to the start of the track.

Track transport is available daily from Tuatapere. All transport must be booked and paid for in advance, and tickets must normally be collected the day before departure. The shuttle departs Tuatapere Information Centre at 7.30 am with accommodation pick-ups available. It should get you on the track for 8 am. On day three it returns from Rarakau Lodge at 3 pm for Tuatapere. This timetable coincides with same-day connections to Te Anau or Queenstown.

If you like, you can avoid walking the first 6 km of the track by taking four-wheel-drive transport to the boundary of Fiordland National Park at Track Burn. This departs Rarakau Lodge at 8 am and returns on day three from Track Burn at 2 pm. This must also be booked through the Tuatapere Hump Ridge Track office.

All track transport can be booked by firing off an email to transport@visitorcentre.co.nz.

DAY ONE

Rarakau to Track Burn
1¾ hours ▪ 6 km

Your welcome to the Tuatapere Hump Ridge Track is a dense coastal forest weaving through lush greenery. The forest floor is carpeted with a profusion of ferns and forest detritus separated from the parent trees by the ubiquitous wind. More ferns are perched on trunks and branches and plaits of supplejack entwine the forest. A dense cloak of mahoe, horopito and kamahi shields the forest from the intense light, and rimu and matai trees protrude through the canopy. Such is the luxuriance of the forest you could mistake it for a tropical jungle.

Descend the steps to the coast through a band of tutu. Cross the Waikoau River 45 minutes from the start on a swingbridge, looking out for the pedestals of a former bridge. The baches near the river are models of Kiwi functionalism – curtains made from old sheets, Vegemite jars as flower vases and outhouses tied down with frayed rope. Cribs as they should be, not showy investment properties decorated to impress the neighbours. These cribs are isolated, in an incomparable setting, not some manufactured 'lifestyle' environment.

Soon you drop down to the beach – and what a beach it is, a lonely expanse of gently shelving sand with a border of rounded pebbles and a thatch of driftwood. The pebbles, derived from the surrounding rock and transported by river or glacier, come in an assortment of colours. The driftwood logs, some of them 10 m long, are in fact tree trunks. Stumps that have evidently been sawn off at the tops of their root systems are now bleached and smoothed by waves. Occasional pebbles have been incorporated into the wood, embedded more elegantly than a human hand could achieve.

> The rails on the beach are left over from an old tramway. In places they have been separated from the coast, the erosive work of several decades' waves gnawing at the mudstone coastline.

Head for the rock cliffs at the far end of the beach. Cross the creek by heading upstream 30 m to a swingbridge. Follow the arrows on the posts to the track behind the beach. The section to the base of the first incline can be boggy, so you may want to make your way back to the beach and cut in over the driftwood and weedy verge.

Not long after you enter the forest, the swingbridge at Track Burn appears (1 hour from Waikoau River).

Track Burn to Flat Creek
45 min ■ 2 km

Cross the swingbridge and enter the forest. Note the large rimu trees, their bark flaking off to thwart epiphytes (the Maori name rimu roughly translates as 'ripple', an allusion to the marking left on the trunk). Silver beech rise over a dense understorey of tree ferns, kamahi and supplejack – unusual components in forests east of the main spine of the Fiordland mountains, where the rainfall is less and the temperatures colder, and vegetation is generally sparser. Here is an exception.

The track undulates through forest, occasionally hovering above sandy bays lapped by waves. The swingbridge over Flat Creek marks the start of the ascent.

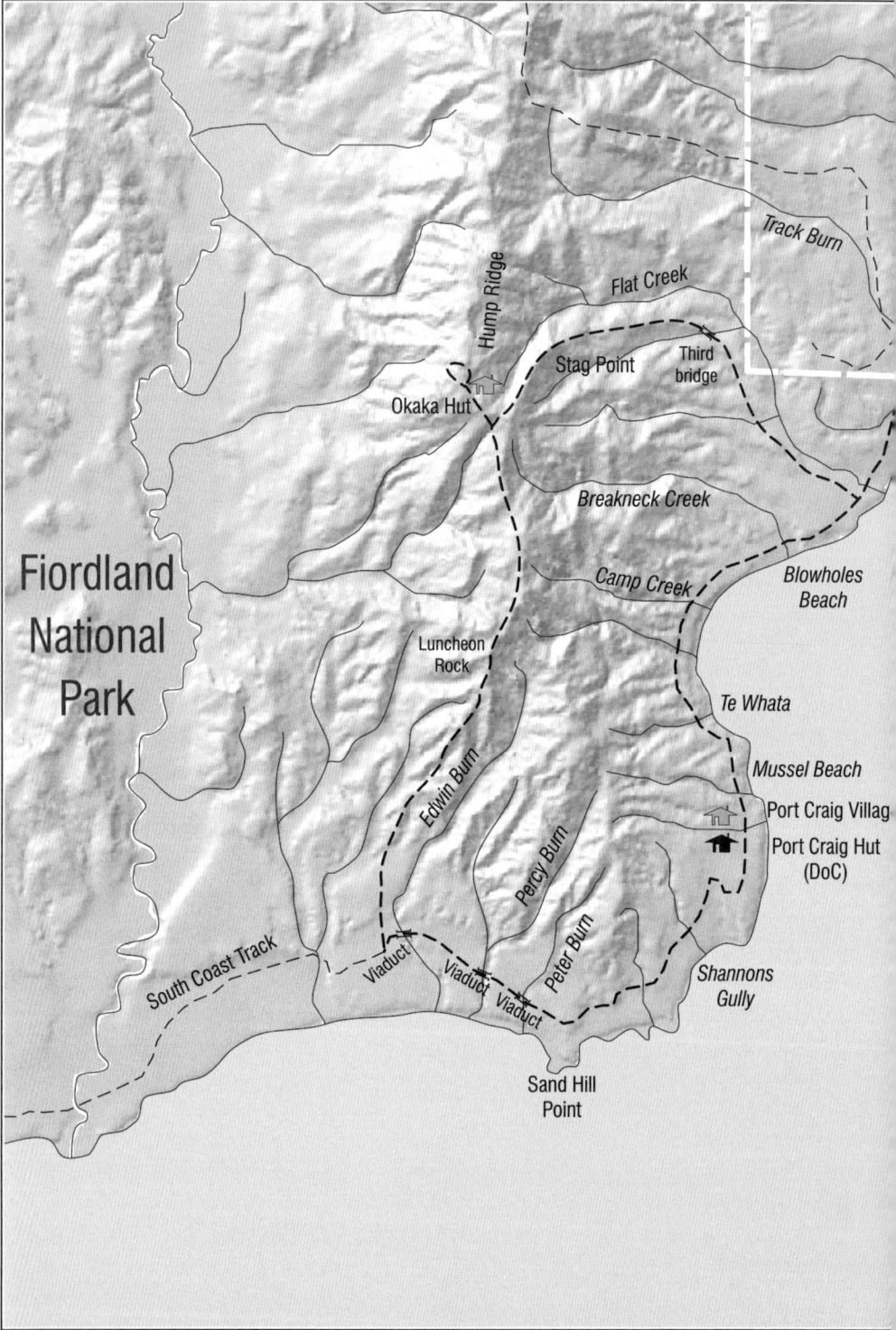

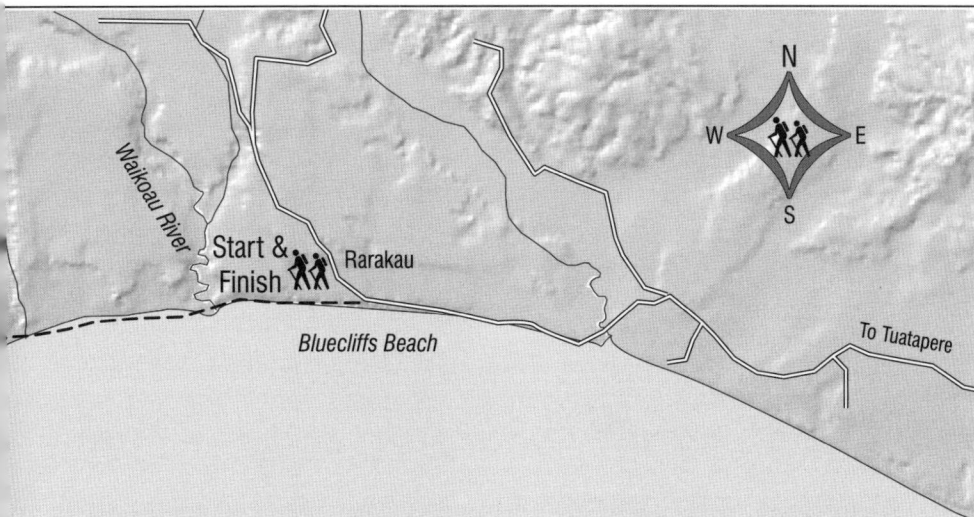

N
W E
S

Waikoau River

Start & Finish

Rarakau

Bluecliffs Beach

To Tuatapere

Te Waewae Bay

TUATAPERE
HUMP RIDGE
TRACK

Key:
🏠 DoC hut
🏠 Private hut
🏠 Shelter
- - - Main track
- - Side track

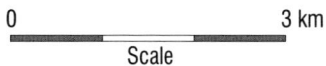

0   3 km

Scale

Flat Creek to third bridge
1¾ hours ■ 4 km

Almost immediately after you cross Flat Creek, the Hump Ridge Track is signposted on the right. A short and sometimes muddy section through the forest leads to the start of the first 2.5 km stretch of a total of 11 km of boardwalk on the track. You start to climb to the crest of a spur clothed in beech forest with a sparse understorey studded with crown ferns and carpeted in moss.

Cross the first swingbridge (45 minutes) and continue along the boardwalk. Look for embracing trees, an unusual combination of two trees that cross over mid-trunk in arboreal intimacy and for the exposed roots that show the shallow rooting depth of the beech trees. Tomtits and fantails flit about the airy interior.

An hour later (having crossed another wooden bridge) there is a third bridge over an unnamed creek. Here some thoughtful soul has tied a billy to a length of twine so trampers can drop it into the stream to refill their water bottles. This is the last of the fresh water before the ascent, so stock up.

Third bridge to Stag Point
2¼ hours ■ 4 km

Now starts the real ascent. Choose your footing carefully on the roots that criss-cross the track. Try to find a rhythm, keep a steady pace and pick an economical route.

After around 1¼ hours the forest starts to change character. Mingimingi, with its fleshy white berries and spiky leaves, enters the mix. In response to the harsher conditions the crown ferns diminish in stature and the new growth is lighter. The bark of the silver beech is encrusted with foliose lichens and a dark green filmy fern lines the trackside. Occasionally Hall's totara, with crooked branches and red bark, make an appearance.

Around 30 minutes before reaching Stag Point, the track reaches its steepest section, surmounting a bluff on the side of the ridge. On the top, the vegetation becomes noticeably more stunted. Stag Point is marked by a sign in a small clearing.

Stag Point to Okaka Hut
45 min ■ 3 km

At Stag Point the coastal views, till now tantalisingly masked by foliage, open up. The arc of Te Waewae Bay recedes to Pahia Point and the Southland Plains seem hemmed in by hills and mountains. The first views of Okaka Hut, nestled neatly below the ridgeline in a sheltered hollow, may deceive you into thinking it is closer than it really is. Tired bodies and eager minds have a habit of altering perception.

In this alpine section an almost unbroken boardwalk protects the fragile plant communities, which include *Dracophyllum menziesii*, bog pine, leatherwood and mountain flax.

In the clear alpine light, take a look south at the Hump Ridge, with occasional boardwalks on the summit ridge. This is tomorrow's route. The Hump Ridge commands more extensive views than other ranges in Fiordland's tightly squeezed valley systems. Closer examination of the rock reveals its sandy granular structure, the mark of a sedimentary rock uplifted and sculpted by wind and rain. It is an uplifted block of sandstone, forming a horst – a block of rock being squeezed up between two faults like a pip between two fingers.

Okaka Hut is soon signposted to the right, the boardwalk weaving down the side of the gully. The hut complex centres on a large kitchen/dining area with padded chairs and a fire. The spacious balconies look out to vast views. Accommodation is provided in two blocks with bunk rooms for six and a corridor with separate toilet blocks.

Summit walk
45 min ▪ 3 km return

This boardwalked loop, an add-on to the main Hump Ridge Track, explores the tops of the Hump Ridge. You should be on this track both in the evening and the following morning for the best visual treats.

The scenery here encapsulates the Hump Ridge. Rock outcrops called tors litter the tops. The bizarre forms are created when weaknesses and cracks in the rock are eroded, leaving the more resistant rock exposed. These are then shaped by wind, rain and frost to the convoluted forms on show. Some are leaning, often with overhangs, but each is a unique piece of art, a combination of Nature's elements at play. Tarns mottle this surreal landscape, occupying poorly drained hollows on flatter sections. Wind ripples the water with every gust but in periods of calm, especially in the early morning, glassy surfaces reflect rock and sky.

The sandstone tors house a distinctive flora. These include *Pimelea crosby-smithiana*, a small shrub with white flowers, and *Olearia crosby-smithiana*. Other notable species include *Hebe canterburiensis*, the nearest other population of which is on the West Coast.

On the western side of the track the vast panoramas are reserved for views of the southern Fiordland mountains and Lake Poteriteri. Lake Hauroko, the deepest lake in New Zealand at 462 m, is shielded to the north. Its name translates as 'soughing or moaning of the wind', an echo of the northerly gales that funnel through the mountain passes.

Snow-capped peaks step towards Preservation Inlet and north towards Mt Titiroa. The perspective to the south over the Waitutu marine terraces is about the best you'll get. The steps in the land are decipherable, rising inland in response to tectonic uplift and marine transgression. At stable sea levels the wave action erodes a cliff in exactly the same way the coastline of today is worked. Earth movements then uplift the block of land for the process to be repeated and a new terrace to be formed.

The 13 terraces of Waitutu represent over 1 million years of tectonic uplift and were added to Fiordland National Park in 1999. In marked contrast to the rest of the park, the terraces have never been glaciated. Above 300 m there is beech forest but below this altitude is lowland podocarp forest, with rimu and kahikatea prominent. Beech is completely absent from the lower terraces.

Following the methodical logging of New Zealand's other lowland podocarp forests, the value of the rimu in the Waitutu area increased. The Maori owners, who had been granted the land in 1906, struck various deals with logging companies but, after pressure from the Royal Forest and Bird Protection Society, the Crown negotiated a land swap and $13.5 million payout in return for managing the land as if it were national park. This protection was consummated in legislation in 1997.

DAY TWO

Okaka Hut to Luncheon Rock

2¼ hours ■ 6 km

This section takes in the most expansive and memorable views of the tramp. You should plan your trip to maximise your chances of catching fine weather for this morning.

From the hut, retrace your steps for 20 minutes to the junction and rejoin the main track. For the most part, the route follows a boardwalk along the ridge, although there are muddy sections too. The track occasionally drops into forest of stunted silver beech trees with mossy cushions on the trunks, their contorted branches forming a uniformly high canopy. Some trunks have gaping apertures – curiously these trees are still alive.

In clearings cushion plants cover the ground and flowering gentians glisten in the sun. Further along the ridge Lake Poteriteri and the Waitutu terraces come into view, giving another chance to appreciate the immense size of the lowland forest of the south coast. The Solander Islands, the least modified offshore islands in New Zealand, jut out of the sea like knuckles 40 km off the coast.

Don't get too carried away with the view in front of you. There is still joy to be had from glancing behind at the ascending ridge and tors.

About 20 minutes before Luncheon Rock there is a large tor to the left of the track, seemingly the last outcrop before the track disappears from view along the ridge. Take a quick detour to the top (mind the edge – the only thing to catch a fall is the ground). Life's most difficult decision at this point is which way to look. Fiordland mountains or Te Waewae Bay? Te Waewae Bay or Fiordland mountains? Looking carefully to the coast you should be able to make out the buildings of the old school house and Port Craig Village. The rock actually arches over the track after its viewpoint, giving a good chance to see the rock's composition – mainly rounded pebbles in a sand matrix – likely deposited at a river mouth before compaction and uplift.

The track descends via steps to where the ridge divides, the track taking the right fork. Luncheon Rock is visible on the ridgeline. Keep an eye to the right and see if you can see the feature known as the Frog. It's easy to spot if you know it's there. Look also for a first glimpse of the viaducts you'll be traversing after lunch.

Stop at Luncheon Rock for a drink, a smoko or a snack. Whatever your excuse, linger for a while to enjoy the last of the big views. The toilet and water tap are a little further on.

> Solander Island rises 340 m and covers 100 hectares. It is an eroded andesite volcano surrounded by stacks and islets. It has peaty soils and a harsh climate. Botanists have recorded 55 vascular plants and five woody species there, including *Olearia lyallii*, a tree daisy that grows to 6 m tall, and the megaherb *Stilbocarpa lyallii*.
>
> There are 38 sea bird species that breed on the island, including 4000 to 5000 pairs of southern Buller's mollymawk (50 per cent of the known population). The southernmost breeding population of the Australasian gannet is often seen gliding on the updraughts.

Although the descent from the ridge is rarely steep, it is often muddy. Note the change in forest composition and temperature as you go. Rimu starts to reappear and kamahi and crown ferns smother the forest floor again. As you lose altitude, the forest cover also becomes thicker.

At the base of the hill the track enters land owned by the descendants of Rachel Matilda Hassall; the right of way is ensured by the Maori trustees. The rusty waters of the Edwin Burn and the coprosmas, kamahi

Luncheon Rock to Edwin Burn viaduct
2½ hours ▪ 5 km

and manuka announce the junction with the South Coast Track and the Edwin Burn viaduct. Turn left.

Edwin Burn viaduct to Peter Burn viaduct
20 min ■ 1.5 km

A glance at the steeply incised mudstone valley carved by the Edwin Burn reveals the height of the viaduct, 22 m above the river. It is an impressive engineering feat and the structure has withstood the brutal weather well. The Edwin Burn viaduct is 50 m long.

The track continues along the route of a tramline that once stretched 17 km from Port Craig to the Waitutu forest. It is not far to the Percy Burn viaduct, built by the Chester Construction Company in 1925 (although the plaque would have you believe it was 1923). This viaduct is 125 m long, 36 m high and built of Australian hardwood. Why import timber when you have one of the most plentiful supplies of timber you could

PORT CRAIG

The Marlborough Timber Company had done rather well out of sawmilling the Opouri Valley up to 1914 and was looking for new opportunities. Daniel Reese, former New Zealand cricketer, and John Craig, an enigmatic yet practical man, were given the task of finding the forest that was going to sustain the company's profits for decades to come.

Craig was sent to the Pacific coast of the USA to see how they did things there. 'Large-scale' and 'modern' were the buzz words he returned with and the search was on to find somewhere these grand plans could become real. Craig, Reese and James Collins, a government timber ranger, spent two weeks exploring the western end of Te Waewae Bay. They ventured along the coast to Sand Hill Point and all the way inland to the edge of Lake Hauroko. Reese estimated there was 500 million feet (1.2 million cubic metres) of timber there for the taking.

With dollars on the insides of their eyelids they waxed lyrical on the splendid forest reserves to the board of directors. Their only reservation was the lack of harbour facilities, a problem they reckoned could be overcome with the construction of a breakwater at Mussel Beach. The board took a field trip and had a jolly old time camping, shooting, drinking and basking in an unusually fine period of Fiordland weather, but making only a cursory inspection of the bush.

By 1917 work was under way on constructing a wharf and orders were put in for equipment to be shipped from the USA, including a Lidgerwood overhead logging plant. The mill was relocated from Opouri. Then, just as the operation was ready to crank up, disaster struck. Craig, in a moment of impetuousness, decided to battle a rising swell and southerly gale to fetch the last piece of plant needed for the boiler. Both Craig and boatman Fred Parry were drowned. After this tragic event Mussel Beach was given its alternative name, Port Craig.

As it was wartime, there was no difficulty finding buyers for the timber. But first the breakwater had to be built to shield the bay from the tempestuous southerlies. Initial budgets wish for all around you? The answer lies in the resistance of some Australian hardwoods to degradation in the wet climes – they tend to be impregnated with natural oils and thus much more stoical in the face of moisture.

The Percy Burn viaduct is a truly impressive structure, testimony to the vision of the industrialists who first mooted the idea and the ingenuity of the men who built it. For it to be in such good nick nearly 100 years after the first post was raised is remarkable. It is said to be the highest wooden viaduct in the world, but dimensional bragging aside, it's a wonder the thing still stands. It spans a deep ravine carved by the Percy Burn into the easily eroded mudstone. A series of posts in several tiers forms the supports, with bracing timbers and steel plates.

Despite the integrity of the design and construction, in the 1990s

of £20,000 were quintupled to £100,000 and a reckless attitude to the cheque book started. The milled timber was sent to Bluff for export or shipping around New Zealand.

On 22 September 1921 the official opening of a new sawmill occurred with much pomp and ceremony. By this time the hefty Lidgerwood log hauler was accomplishing its task in the surrounding forest. The machine used a 36 m vertical spar to winch logs from the bush to waiting tram bogies. Once the radius of the hauler had been exhausted of timber, the Lidgerwood was winched onto locomotives and taken along the tramline to a new site. The extreme weight necessitated heavy-duty foundations, sleepers, rails and viaducts.

Life at Port Craig was Spartan. It was a company town – the company paid the wages and provided the housing, meals, goods in the shops and leisure activities. The Port Craig settlement was New Zealand's first cashless settlement, with the cost of items procured from the stores deducted from weekly wages. Schooling was carried out at the town school, the roll peaking in 1921 at 35 pupils as the workforce increased to around 200.

Mill manager Peter Daly, tough, intelligent and fair, was just the character needed to overcome the logistical, technical and motivational issues of this isolated and wild place. He knew that many timber towns had failed in the wake of alcohol-fuelled fights, disputes and loss of productivity. He therefore sanctioned the imbibing of alcohol only on Saturday nights, when the weekly dance was held and, fearful of upsetting the ladies, the men would moderate their behaviour.

By 1928 a lull in the timber market was having a disastrous effect on profits. The massive overheads involved in sustaining such large machinery meant the operation was no longer viable and the plant was shut down and the town evacuated. It was not until the late 1930s that the plant was finally removed, so ending the largest sawmilling operation in the southern hemisphere.

engineering assessments put the future of the viaducts in question. Around $350,000 was needed to keep them safe and open and the Tuatapere community rallied round to find the cash. The Armstrong Rigging Company carried out the repairs to the three viaducts, adding handrails, putting strengtheners on the rotting posts and bearers and replacing braces and metalwork where necessary.

While walking the deck, take a look at the tree ferns below. It's not often you get to see the radiating fronds from above. On the far side of the viaduct is Mick's Hut, named after Mick Eason, 'a big man with a big heart'. He dreamed of a hut for all to use and set out on a personal mission to construct one here. The hut was completed in 1998, but Mick died soon after. As he intended, the hut is there for all to use, but please respect the premises and leave a donation at the Tuatapere service station. There are 18 bunks, a wood burner and table, and toilets.

About 10 minutes further on is the Peter Burn (or Sand Hill) viaduct, 17 m high and 59 m long. This is the final one of the remarkable trio of viaducts.

Peter Burn viaduct to Port Craig
2 hours ■ 6.5 km

The old tramline is still in a very good state, although this becomes less surprising when you consider it was built to railway standard to transport the 80-ton Lidgerwood hauler over bush terrain. The sleepers are numerous, many having rotted little in the waterlogged conditions. Steel pins still jut out occasionally and the gravel substrate often ponds water. Most muddy sections are deceptively shallow, but a few sections, especially in the dank cuttings, are boot-deep in mud. Savvy trampers have trodden an alternative path for the worst sections. The waterlogged conditions are also evidenced by the sphagnum colonies, some raised above the trackside. Sometimes you feel you are squelching rather than tramping.

Some of the cuttings show the cross-section of the root systems, which reach out over the hillside like the tentacles of an octopus. The forest at the track edge is mainly regenerating kamahi as well as manuka that sometimes reach over the track like ecclesiastical arches.

Cross the swingbridge at Shannons Gully before reaching the old school house at Port Craig (DoC hut) or continue another few metres to the Hump Ridge Track Port Craig Village complex.

DoC has constructed a metalled trail that explores the relics of the sawmill operations at Port Craig. A free leaflet available from the information board near the school house or at Port Craig Village fills in the details about a series of numbered sites.

Port Craig Heritage Trail
45 min ▪ 2 km return

Among the more interesting relics are the cement barrels. The cement was stored in wooden barrels that have rotted away to leave the form of the barrels – the mould has gone but the fill remains. Also worth a look are the concrete trough used as a repository for nine toilet stalls, the partially restored brick boiler house still smelling of smoke, the slag heap of the blacksmith's shop, the hulk of the wharf crane still smelling of oil, the bed plate of the hauler and the remaining wharf piles. Other detritus includes rusting boilers, rock wagons, cables, wheels, water tanks and rain heads.

DAY THREE

Backtrack 50 m to the school house and follow the sign to the car park. Don't let this even, metalled track lull you into a false sense of security for the track to come.

Port Craig to Blowholes Beach
2½ hours ▪ 8 km

The section after Te Whata is pleasantly shaded by a towering but open forest of beech and rimu, with prolific ferns taking advantage of the rainfall. This also contributes to the occasional muddy section, most of which are of stiff consistency rather like thick chocolate mousse. Creeks such as Camp Creek are all bridged, providing viewpoints for the tumbling watercourse below. Mossy boulders, white foaming water and rounded bedrock make attention-grabbing scenes. All the while, the sounds of waves echo through the forest – and before long you will reach the shore at Breakneck Creek, where the pebbles and shells of the beach contrast with the rock platform off the shore.

Blowholes Beach, 5 minutes from Breakneck Beach over a small headland, is a small bay enclosed by forest, with flax bushes and a small creek to complete the picture. Low tide exposes rock pools and beds of pink seaweed, and the enticing blue waters and golden sand summon visions of the tropics. On a fine day you may have to pinch yourself to remember this is the south coast of Fiordland. This is definitely your lunch spot. Stewart Island is bang ahead in the view.

Blowholes Beach to Flat Creek
45 min ▪ 2 km

The track continues around the headland to a marker on a rock at the far end of the beach, where the track heads inland over small promontories to the next equally idyllic beach, secluded and worthy of a lingering stop. The pattern is repeated to a final beach before the return to Flat Creek and the junction with the Hump Ridge Track, where you were the day before yesterday.

Flat Creek to Rarakau
2½ hours ▪ 8 km

At low tide return to Rarakau via Bluecliffs Beach, an open expanse in view of the Hump Ridge that allows contemplation of your previous few days. It was only yesterday you were up there on the ridge. There's also time to look forward to your shower, beer and comfy sofa. It has been a big three days.

KEPLER TRACK

66 km ■ four days ■ loop ■ Great Walk

The Kepler Track is a Great Walk on a good track surface, starting and finishing near Te Anau. Every year around 8000 trampers enjoy the beech forest, alpine views, caves and lakeshore beaches.

On day one the walk follows the shore of Lake Te Anau from the DoC visitor centre. The true start of the track is reached at the control gates, which regulate the flow of the Upper Waiau River. The track leaves the lake shore at Brod Bay, a stunning sandy beach, and begins a climb through beech forest to the bushline and expansive views of the Kepler Mountains and South Fiord. The first night is spent at Luxmore Hut looking towards the northern reaches of the lake.

Day two is spent mostly on the tops, with the high point being the ascent of Mt Luxmore. Back on the main track, a gentle climb with changing views leads to a knife-edge arête, a traverse not for the vertiginous. After a lookout over the entire glaciated Iris Burn Valley, it's a steep zigzag descent to the valley floor and Iris Burn Hut.

Day three is almost entirely in beech forest to the flats alongside the Iris Burn. After Rocky Point the track approaches Lake Manapouri, the idyllic sands of Shallow Bay and Moturau Hut. Those tramping over four days rest here for the night. Rainbow Reach, where you can get transport back to Te Anau, is a further 2 hours away.

Day four passes the Amoeboid Mire on the way to the Waiau River, then heads upstream to the control gates. Trampers get the shuttle back to Te Anau or walk the final 45 minutes back to their accommodation.

The idea for the Kepler Track was first proposed by prominent Te Anau locals, including Les Henderson and Alf Hexall, as a way to celebrate Fiordland National Park's centennial in 1988. The idea to build a loop walk with easy public access without the need for a boat was high on the agenda of the Fiordland National Park Board. Investigations started in the summer of 1985. Chief ranger Paul Green, along with John Ombler, John Trotter and Tom Patterson, walked to Mt Luxmore, following a track originally cut by deer cullers. They walked over the Keplers on a beautiful sunny day, tracing roughly the route of today's track and dropped into the Iris Burn. They were sold on the idea.

Construction of the section from Rainbow Reach to the control gates was overseen by long-time ranger Ken Bradley. The section to Shallow Bay was completed under the employment scheme as a way of keeping unemployed workers busy. After a full survey was carried out, construction of the main track began in 1986. Much of the work was carried out by Operation Raleigh volunteers. A small digger (in four parts) and a mechanical barrow were flown in, the first time mechanical plant had been used in track construction in the region. The official opening took place late in 1988.

The popularity of the walk has slowly escalated, spurred along by the annual Kepler Challenge, usually held in early December. The event involves around 400 competitors running a 60 km circuit. Many come from overseas and around New Zealand, but a healthy number are Southland locals. The winning time for a walk that takes some people four days? Under 5 hours!

As you walk the section of the Kepler Track from the base of the Iris Burn to the control gates, spare a thought for the thousands of protestors who ensured it is not a ghost forest of decaying trees drowned for the benefit of a foreign corporate to make more money. When in the 1960s the idea of building an aluminium smelter in New Zealand was first mooted, one of the main reasons Tiwai Point in Bluff was chosen as the location was the hydroelectric potential of nearby Lakes Manapouri and

Te Anau. With mean lake levels of around 180 m and 200 m respectively, and a distance of only 10 km to sea level at Doubtful Sound, coupled with prodigious rainfall, the lakes were an obvious source of energy to power the massive new plant.

The first plan involved raising the level of Lake Manapouri by as much as 30 m, but this preposterous suggestion was toned down to an 8 m rise. Seventeen islands would be submerged and the beaches drowned, a ribbon of decaying forest would scar the edge and wetlands would be flooded. In 1969 local residents set up in impassioned opposition to the proposal. The Save Manapouri Campaign became New Zealand's first nationwide environmental movement, and a petition with more than 265,000 signatures was delivered to Parliament. The campaign was ultimately successful – in 1972 the newly elected Labour government ruled out raising the water levels at all.

SECTION TIMINGS

DAY ONE   6 hours 16.5 km

Te Anau to control gates	50 min	3 km
Control gates to Brod Bay	1½ hours	5.5 km
Brod Bay to Luxmore Hut	3½ hours	8 km

DAY TWO   6 hours 14.5 km

Luxmore Hut to Mt Luxmore	1¾ hours	3 km
Mt Luxmore to Forest Burn Shelter	30 min	2 km
Forest Burn Shelter to Hanging Valley Shelter	1½ hours	3.5 km
Hanging Valley Shelter to Iris Burn Hut	2 hours	6 km

DAY THREE   4½ hours 16.5 km

Iris Burn Hut to Rocky Point	2¼ hours	8.5 km
Rocky Point to Moturau Hut	2 hours	8 km

DAY FOUR   5½ hours 18.5 km

Moturau Hut to Rainbow Reach	1¾ hours	6 km
Rainbow Reach to control gates	3 hours	9.5 km
Control gates to Te Anau	50 min	3 km

BOOKING

As this is a DoC Great Walk, all accommodation, both huts and camping, must be booked in advance (www.doc.govt.nz). There are three huts on the tramp (Luxmore Hut 55 bunks, Iris Burn Hut 50 bunks, Moturau Hut 40 bunks). Campsites are at Brod Bay, Iris Burn and Shallow Bay, making day two a biggie with about 23 km of walking, an ascent of more than 1000 m and a descent of more than 700 m.

Terralink's Milford & Kepler Tracks map is the best for this area. DoC's Kepler Trackmap 335-09 is also available.

GETTING THERE

The beauty of the Kepler is that it's a loop starting and finishing within walking distance of Te Anau. The purists' way of completing the track would be to walk out of your front door to the start of the track and arrive back to your accommodation on foot also. On day one, walking from your accommodation to Luxmore Hut is very satisfying.

The start of the track proper is through the control gates at the entrance to Fiordland National Park. By car, follow SH 95 2.3 km from the junction with SH 94 at the Fiordland National Park Visitor Centre and turn right into Golf Course Road (Kepler Track is signposted). After 2.3 km turn right along a short road that leads to the car park. You will need to head upstream for 5 minutes to reach the control gates. DoC signs warn against leaving your car here – better to use secure parking in Te Anau.

The other entry/exit point of the track is at Rainbow Reach, 11.2 km down SH 95 (Te Anau–Manapouri highway). The Kepler Track is again signposted on the right and a large DoC sign also on the right indicates Rainbow Reach. The unsealed road continues 1.5 km to the parking area by the swingbridge. A shelter and toilet are situated here.

There are a few ways to shorten the walk, taking up to 15 km off the distance and making it possible to complete it in three days.

Kepler Water Taxis runs a daily shuttle service to Brod Bay, which cuts out the first 2½ hours of day one. Water taxis usually leave the boat-hire wharf near the i-Site information centre at 8.30 am and 9.30 am daily

during the Great Walks peak season (end October to end April).
Other departures can be organised by reservation.

Tracknet runs a shuttle bus from Te Anau to the control gates at 8.30 am and 9.30 am, with trips to Rainbow Reach at 9.30 am, 2.30 pm and 4.15 pm. These leave Rainbow Reach at 10 am, 3 pm and 4.30 pm. Shuttles should be booked to confirm a place, but outside busy periods you will probably find there is space if you haven't booked, or if you wish to catch an earlier service.

Other bus companies may also run shuttles, information for which can be obtained at the DoC Fiordland National Park Visitor Centre in Te Anau.

Kepler Water Taxis
0-3-249 8364 or 025 357 361
stevsaunders@xtra.co.nz

Tracknet
0-3-249 7777
0800 483 262
www.tracknet.net

DAY ONE

Not everyone will walk this first section as it's possible to drive to the control gates and the start of the track proper, but if you do, you will be rewarded with views of Jackson Peaks and the Kepler Mountains. In the early morning, tranquil Lake Te Anau with shags feeding from the rocks, tui breakfasting on flax and scaups creating V-shaped wakes is a fine setting in which to embark on your journey.

Te Anau to control gates
50 min ■ 3 km

The route passes through Te Anau Wildlife Centre, where the collection of rare native birds includes takahe in a predator-proof enclosure. It's particularly apt viewing these cheeky rails with the Murchison Mountains as the backdrop. The jagged summits and forested hillsides are their last stronghold in the wild.

Entering the short boardwalk section, take a look along the lake shore, noting the orange-coloured turf communities on the rocks and the swards of oioi behind. You will see this vegetation succession, a key feature of the lake edge, again later in the trip.

As you pass near the site of Henry's Hut at the base of the escarpment, look over your shoulder at the promontory on which Te Anau nestles and the Earl Mountains in the distance. This is a view that will become familiar over the course of the day, although it is ever changing with the increase in altitude.

Notable species of the lake shore include *Cardamine lacustris*, discovered in 1971 by Dunedin botanist Peter Johnson, the buttercup *Ranunculus recens* var. *lacustris* and the threatened *Hydatella inconspicua*. The sedges higher up the shore include *Carex gaudichaudiana* in a belt up to 50 m wide. Jointed rush or oioi grows as high as 1 m and merges with the manuka shrubland bordering the forest.

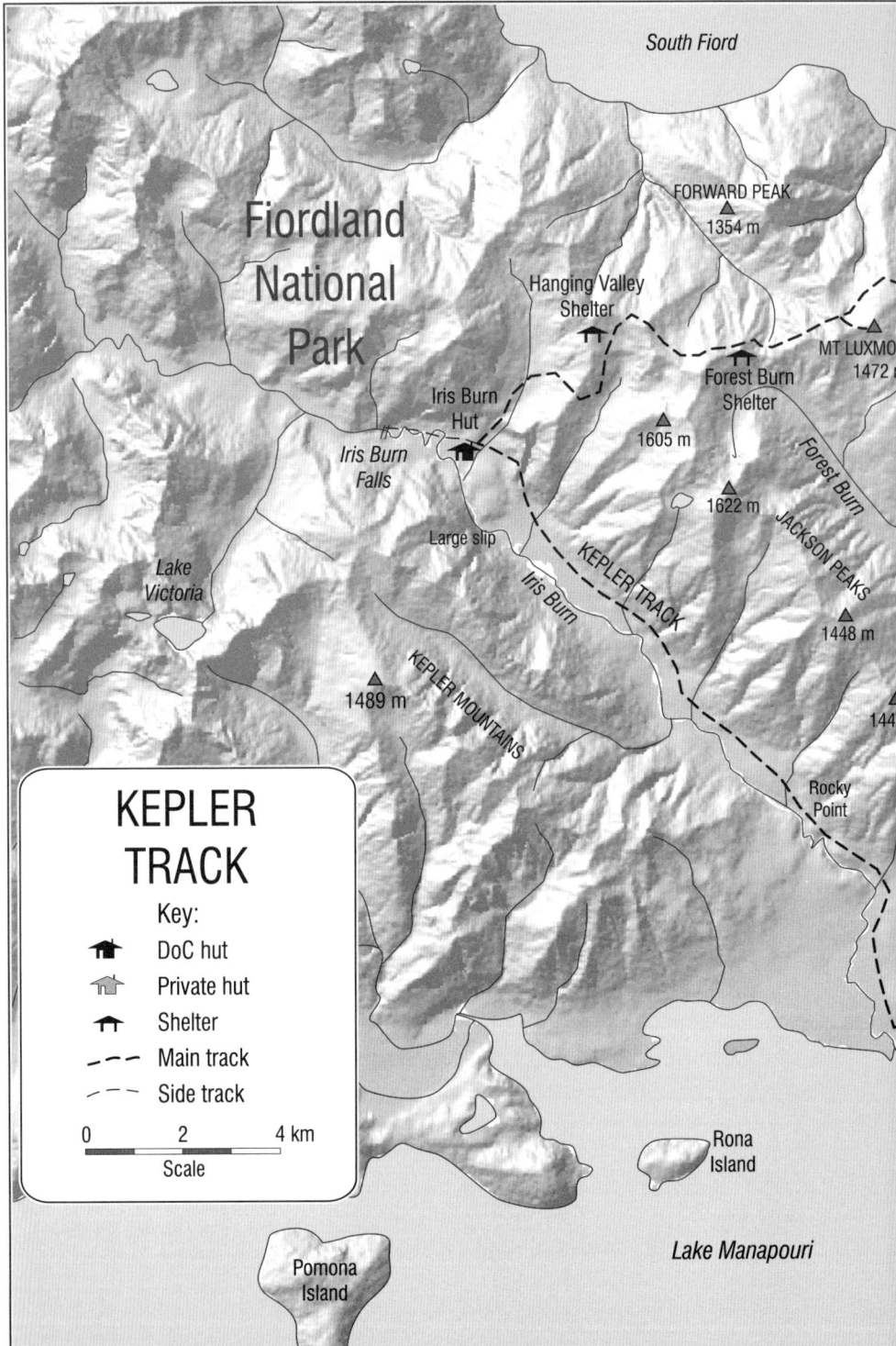

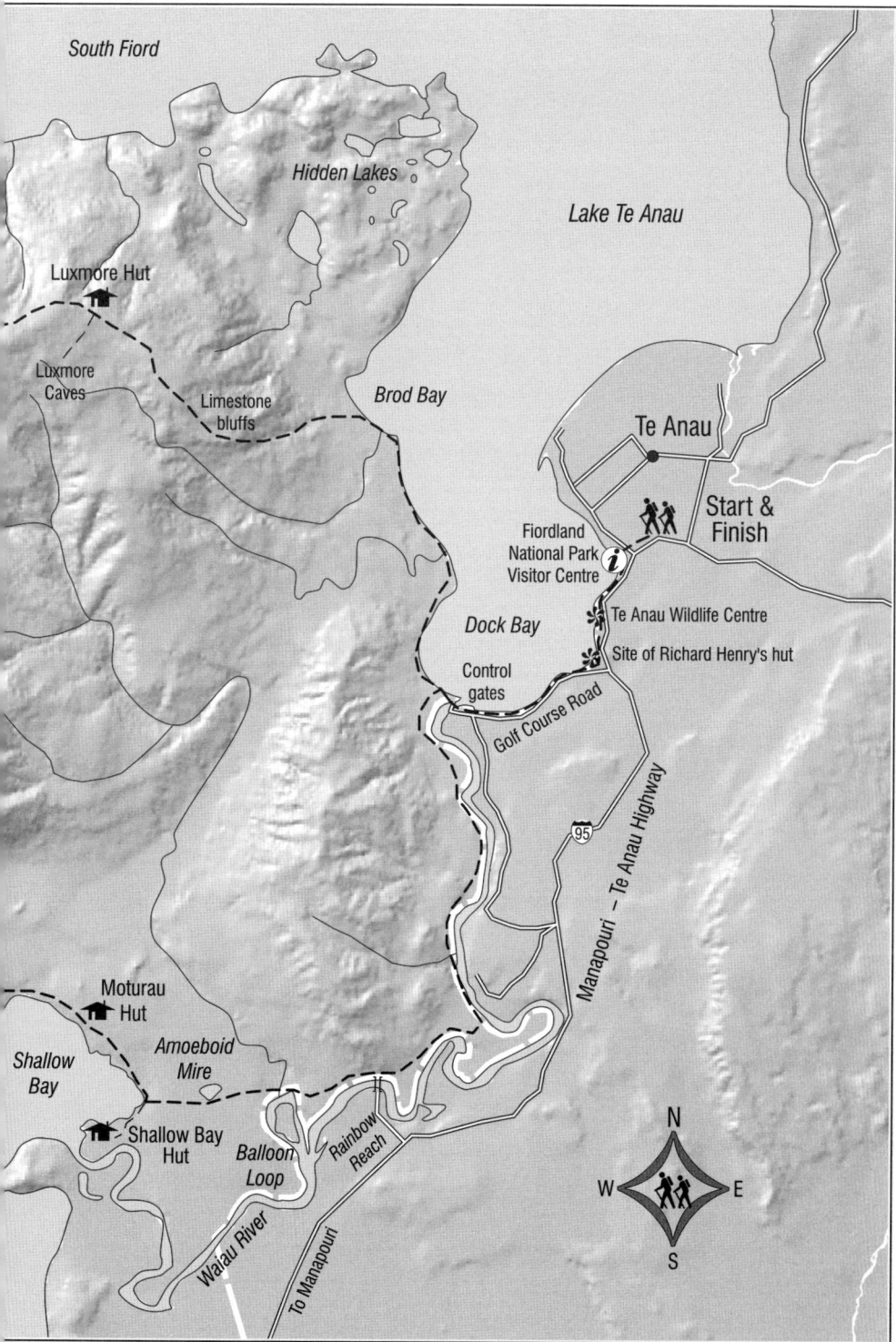

South Fiord

Hidden Lakes

Lake Te Anau

Luxmore Hut

Luxmore
Caves

Limestone
bluffs

Brod Bay

Te Anau

Start &
Finish

Fiordland
National Park
Visitor Centre

i

Te Anau Wildlife Centre

Dock Bay

Site of Richard Henry's hut

Control
gates

Golf Course Road

95

Manapouri – Te Anau Highway

Moturau
Hut

Amoeboid
Mire

Shallow
Bay

Shallow Bay
Hut

Balloon
Loop

Rainbow
Reach

Waiau River

To Manapouri

N

W   E

S

The formidable concrete structures of the control gates manage the outflow of Lake Te Anau into the Waiau River and Lake Manapouri. When you go through the gated fence over the control gates you are entering Fiordland National Park. Take a look over the side at the swirling waters of the river and continue to the sign at the start of the Kepler Track.

Control gates to Brod Bay
1½ hours ▪ 5.5 km

Your welcome to the beech forest is provided by towering silver and mountain beech with a few examples of red beech, all depositing their litter of decaying leaves on the track surface like a walkway of confetti. The track is wide and even. Mountain beech is conspicuous on the lake margins, taking advantage of the cool air that sinks to the lake level and forms a cooler band below the inversion. There is a toilet on the left near the start.

An opening in the forest looks straight up Lake Te Anau, where the dark line of Centre Island contrasts with the misty tones on the snowy peaks at the northern end, the most prominent of them Mt Anau. You're heading towards the bright gravels of Dock Bay, which you will reach after 30 minutes weaving through bird-filled forest. Paradise shelducks make a noisy accompaniment out on the lake.

Take a short walk up Dock Bay around the point (just past the toilet, barbecues and picnic tables). The sound of the relative hurly-burly of Te Anau travels effortlessly over the calm waters from the opposite shore. Ripples concentrate the light through clear water into oscillating shadows of themselves on the shallow bottom of the lake. The small beach terraces are formed by wave action at higher lake levels pushing up a barricade of stones to form a low platform. The patterned pebbles give clues to the geology of the area. Hornblende and mica flakes in the lighter-coloured granodiorite pebbles are most common.

Brod Bay was named after Thomas Brodrick, skipper of *Te Uira*, a passenger vessel on Lake Te Anau in the late 19th century. He was quite a character and used to make his passengers disembark to cut firewood to fuel the boilers. He also had a boat named *Ripple*, which kept breaking down. One night a local painted the letter 'C' in front of the name. Brod hadn't noticed until several trips had been completed and the whole town had a laugh.

Shortly after Dock Bay, cross the footbridge over Coal Creek. The forest floor is smothered in delicate mosses that soften the contours of the rocks, windfalls and roots. Closer examination reveals some are like lace, some hairy and others resemble caterpillars. Sprays of crown ferns decorate the forest floor, but the understorey continues to be sparse, giving the forest an open and airy feel. There are occasional glimpses of the lake through the languid beech branches.

Brod Bay is a delightful spot with a soft sandy beach curving to a gently protruding point. The southern point clearly shows the lakeshore vegetation sequence from turf communities through oioi, manuka and finally beech forest. There are toilets, barbecues, and a picnic and camping area (between yellow pegs), and it is the arrival point of the water taxi. Fill your water bottles from the lake, as this is the last easily accessible water source before Luxmore Hut and it tastes better than the Te Anau town water from the tap.

Brod Bay to Luxmore Hut
3½ hours ■ 8 km

The steady climb to the bushline is relentless but never steep. At first you cross old terraces deposited by the retreating glacier from Te Anau's South Fiord between 14,000 and 7000 years ago. On the lower slopes mountain and silver beech dominate, with a few tree ferns in the understorey. As the altitude increases mountain beech drops out of the mix for a while and silver beech partners the red beech. The moss cover is profuse, sometimes dripping from the vegetation in mats.

After about 1¾ hours there is a small clearing in the canopy. The delicate architecture of beech branches frames a view of Te Anau township and the fertile dairying plains behind. A small rock gives room for one person at a time to rest and snack while taking it all in. It's obvious the town was sited by a northern hemisphere settler unwilling to accept that northern slopes catch the sun in the southern hemisphere, not southern like in Blighty. This situation is changing, with massive subdivisions opening up around 1000 sections on the northern side of the promontory. Unfortunately, the prime locations next to the lake with the sun and views are to be fenced for private dwellings rather than preserved for all to enjoy as public areas.

A further 20 minutes will bring you to the limestone bluffs, which suddenly fill the uphill view. A huge overhang, notched and with a natural seat sculpted at the base, rises so steeply you have to crane your neck to see the top. Some significant bridges and structures line the base of the cliffs, which have small rivulets trickling down and are mantled with a dense mat of moss, taking advantage of the abundant moisture.

The first rock you see is not in fact limestone but gabbro. This green-tinged mudstone is a hard compaction of rock fragments formed around 250 million years ago. The limestone a little further on is more distinctly white and the coral and shell fragments give it a sandy consistency.

A zigzag section continues towards the bushline, which you should reach after 45 minutes. Your impending arrival on the tops is marked by concentrations of silver beech, which become more stunted the higher you go. Old man's beard, a hairy pale-green lichen, adheres to branches and twigs.

The transition into open views at the top is sudden. The twin peaks of Mt Luxmore loom ahead, while a glance behind reveals Lakes Manapouri and Monowai closing off the distant southern horizon. Shortly afterwards,

RARE BIRDS – TWO EARLY IDENTITIES

Richard Henry, the first European settler on the shores of Lake Te Anau, built a 'mansion' of slabs and thatch at the base of a small terrace in the 1880s. Born in Australia and a boat-builder by trade, he took a keen interest in the natural world. To finance his ornithological forays, he worked for local landowners and cruised Lake Te Anau in his diminutive launch *Putangi*. A resourceful, sober, intelligent and self-educated man, he spent evenings studying natural history, only occasionally disturbed by the ringing of the bell attached to the end of a fishing line cast through the window of his hut.

In 1889, accompanied by Robert Murrell of Manapouri, he set out from the Middle Fiord of Lake Te Anau to find a route to George Sound, a sea fiord on the west coast. He returned 26 days later, fait accompli, having traversed a pass that would later be named in his honour.

When in 1894 Resolution Island was established as a sanctuary for flightless birds, Henry was the natural choice as curator and caretaker and he embraced this role for the next 14 years. His passion and love for birds manifested in his painstaking care to save the kakapo from extinction.

John Beer, known to everyone as Jack, was another early European settler. He came to Te Anau from Riverton, apparently fleeing a failed love affair, and farmed the runs beside the Waiau River. As access could be troublesome, he bought a ramshackle punt and crudely attached it to a wire over the river to prevent its being washed downstream.

Beer kept up to 400 sheep on the tops over the summer months and constructed a slab hut just below the bushline as his summer home. The clearing site is just below Luxmore Hut. He cut a track to Mt Luxmore, although this followed a different route to today's. He also kept a property at the mouth of Henry Creek, north of Te Anau, and grazed sheep on land owned by Te Anau Downs Station. He was a squatter, but a blind eye was turned.

Jack Beer was a rough and ready sort of chap, but considered honest and harmless. He would shear a sheep on the spot whenever he managed to catch one and delivered his banded Berkshire pigs to the local guesthouses in a wheelbarrow. He once carried a sack of flour from Te Anau to his main residence at Beers Pool, below the mouth of the Waiau River, only to realise he had carted it in error and he walked all the way back to return it.

He was found dead in his hut one morning in 1930, aged 70, probably smelling little different from when he was alive.

as you reach the domed apex of the ridge, the view north opens up. On the other side of Lake Te Anau are the innumerable peaks of the Livingstone, Eyre and Takitimu Mountains.

Boardwalked sections have been constructed to protect the fragile peat bog that has formed on the poorly drained soils of the tops. Following the end of the last ice age, water accumulated in the hollows and specialised plant communities developed. The darker water mottles the pastel vegetation in places on the flatter parts of the tops, sometimes around slumps.

Glaciation was also responsible for the smoothed-out hollows of the Hidden Lakes, so named because they remain concealed until you are above them, as well as the kame terraces following the contour line below Mt Luxmore's east peak. These slopes were used as a ski field in the 1970s, with keen amateurs lugging a rope tow up the track you've just walked. The operation didn't last long.

The alpine vegetation on the tops makes an interesting mosaic. Most prominent on the way to Luxmore Hut is the mountain daisy with its large, leathery leaves around the base of the flowers, sometimes appearing in multitudes around the same plant. The hairy tomentum on the back of the leaves traps air close to the leaf to conserve moisture. On hot summer days you can see why this feature has evolved. The overwhelmingly dominant tussock is the mop-like spirals of curly snow tussock. The *Dracophyllum* genus prevalent is a brownish rusty plant with spiky leaves and red tips. Also known as turpentine plant, it burns well when wet and dry. More diminutive and less noticeable are mountain buttercups, mountain violets and St John's wort.

This section from the bushline undulates gently on its way to Luxmore Hut, which only becomes visible after you round the corner into the shallow gully in which it nestles. The true Mt Luxmore peak, distinguished by a trig at the summit, comes into view.

While you're at the hut it's worth making the signposted detour to the Limestone Caves. Take note of the sign at the entrance, including the request to 'cave softly'. A torch is essential, although the advice is to have two per person. If you're not sure of the state of the batteries, then take spares. You should also write your intentions in the hut book and try to go with at least one other person. You can delve around 800 m into the cave, almost 45 minutes if you're game, and if you get in trouble it's a struggle to get you out. Be safe.

The limestone in the caves is the compacted remains of a reef system that once lay in shallow warm waters. Tectonic uplift has resurfaced the rock, which is mainly composed of calcareous matter derived from the shellfish, fish and coral organisms. Limestone is susceptible to dissolving if the water passing through it is acid from the absorption of carbon dioxide in the atmosphere. The percolating groundwater creates fissures that streams can later exploit to form cave systems.

It's very sad to see the broken stalactites near the entrance, snapped off as souvenirs. Even a short stem can take a human lifetime to build up, so this damage impinges on three generations of future visitors. Give your boots a little spring clean on entering the stream at the entrance and try to keep mud out of clean areas. In some places you will have to squeeze past rocks and crawl on hands and knees, but the display of intricate calcite formations is fascinating.

Back above ground, look over to the Murchisons, where the triangular faces of truncated spurs indicate where ridges have been severed by a bulldozing glacier. There is also a classic example of a hanging valley high above the main valley and hemmed in by the pyramid peaks and ridges of the accumulation zone.

A cursory exploration below the hut reveals a small clearing, site of Jack Beer's alpine hut. Old man's beard hangs from the branches of silver beech like bunting, a sign of the air's purity. A large gall, caused by a fungus, clings to the side of a beech tree. These galls are prized by woodturners for fashioning bowls with interesting grain patterns.

Luxmore Hut (1085 m) has 40 bunks in two rooms with a large communal area looking north-east over the South Fiord and the Murchison Mountains. The large decks miss the evening sun but welcome the first rays of dawn, with the odd mischievous kea to wake you by sliding down the roof at daybreak.

DAY TWO

Luxmore Hut to Mt Luxmore
1¾ hours ■ 3 km

When you set off on day two, make sure you take plenty of water with you, as you will not be able to refill your bottle until near the end of today's walk.

From behind the hut the track begins a steady ascent in the shadow of Mt Luxmore's east peak. The rusty rock is ultramafic, with high concentrations of iron, weathered on the exterior surface to the familiar colour of rusty oxidised iron. The nutrient-deficient soils developing on the parent rock are thin and support little life, hence the exposure of the rocks to weathering and rapid down-slope movement. The precipitous walls of the terminus of South Fiord make a brief appearance. Entering a small glaciated gully notable for its steep headwall, small stream and alpine bogs, you gain the clearest vista of both west and east peaks and the juncture of the rock types. The west peak with the trig is much lighter in colour and composed of diorite.

The track starts a steeper ascent and heads around the back of Mt Luxmore. This is accompanied by the opening up of a different set of views, dominated by Coronation Peak, a hummocky summit standing proud of its neighbours on the horizon. The snaking continuation of the track threads around the mountainside.

The signposted detour to the summit of Mt Luxmore (1472 m, 20 minutes return) scrambles over the exposed outcrops of diorite and granite to the trig at the summit. The satisfaction of attaining a peak adds to the tramp's experience. Mt Luxmore seems to stand in isolation from all other peaks except nearby Jackson Peaks, separated by the Forest Burn Valley. Looking north, Forward Peak hides the terminus of South Fiord, with Mt Irene dominant on the horizon. To the far north you can even just make out Mt Madeline in the Darran Mountains.

In summer flying insects and grasshoppers abound. They take advantage of the short but intense summer to feed and breed.

Mt Luxmore to Forest Burn Shelter
30 min ■ 2 km

Descend Mt Luxmore the same way and turn left on rejoining the main track. As you round Forward Peak the views of South Fiord's terminus open up again. Framed in the foreground by descending ridges and highlighted at the rear by the snowline, this is one of the scenic highlights of the tramp. The track hugs the hillside ahead of you and at times disappears, as if becoming part of the view itself.

Ground-hugging cushion plants include *Raoulia* species. Whipcord hebes, obvious because of their closely packed opposite leaves and resemblance to a whipcord, frequently grow in partnership with small speargrass. Look out for the black mountain ringlet butterflies, which float about like flaky paper embers from a fire.

Approaching Forest Burn Shelter (1270 m) you can see the shelter has been bolted down with solid steel strips – it is subject to vicious winds howling over the ridgeline.

Forest Burn Shelter to Hanging Valley Shelter

1½ hours ▪ 3.5 km

A little way past Forest Burn Shelter a pronounced cleft in the rock marks an active fault line. Looking down the valley towards South Fiord the stream capture is evident. The fault line has 'captured' the watercourse, which now flows down the same path as the fault. Beyond the fault the rocks are harder granite, with smoother contours and whitish colour where slips have removed the soil. There's a noticeable change in vegetation too. Buttercups have colonised the shattered exposed rocks near the fault and more hebes enter the mix.

The track passes some exposed granite outcrops that tumble to oblivion below. These are good points to linger before the climb to the saddle. Near the saddle South Fiord becomes partially obscured, but along the saddle new views open up to the south. A small bowl ringed with slumps is studded with tarns, while the steep triangular faces of the upper Iris Burn guard the rear.

The route now hugs the ridgeline of the saddle, skirting the forest before arriving at the Hanging Valley Shelter (1390 m). It is clear how the shelter received its name – it has excellent views, especially to the south, of hanging valleys left behind by the retreating ice.

Hanging Valley Shelter to Iris Burn Hut

2 hours ▪ 6 km

The track descends a knife-edge arête between two valleys. A brief view of the zigzags you are about to descend appears on the right.

Before embarking on the descent, take the 10-minute return detour to the lookout at the end of the ridge before it plunges valleyward. This gives a picture of the Iris Burn from top to toe. To the west are Iris Burn Falls and the debris-filled valley at the foot of steep walls. Downstream, past the Big Slip, the mouth of the burn enters Shallow Bay and Lake Manapouri, framed by forested mountainsides.

A curious trio of coniferous shrubs forms a band above the forest. Pygmy pine, bog pine and celery pine cower low to the ground, forming dense canopies with dracophyllum. After a day on the tops it's a welcome change to re-enter the beech forest, especially on a hot summer's day when the sun can be scorching on the exposed ridges. Foliose lichens grow in profusion, with old man's beard dangling everywhere. In places you cannot see the wood for the lichen. Prickly shield fern, rough to the touch, coats the forest floor.

Innumerable track zigzags take you to the stream at the base of the valley, which is crossed by a footbridge. Moss-encrusted boulders fill the streambed and languid beech branches, festooned in moss, drip overhead. This is the first opportunity to refill your water bottles since Luxmore Hut.

On the other side of the stream a sign warns of rockfall, which is especially likely in heavy rain. You will soon arrive at a small lookout on a footbridge with views down the valley of the Big Slip, which is still early in the process of recolonisation by vegetation. You are now below the lip of the hanging valley and entering the main Iris Burn Valley. The light green, heart-shaped, serrated leaves of the mountain ribbonwood are a harmonious addition to the darker forest hues. Mosses start to colonise the bare surfaces in mats of green.

A short detour to a waterfall is signposted on the right, although it only musters a mere trickle except after rain. A few more zigzags lead through the airy forest to Iris Burn Hut (498 m) on the valley floor. In front of the hut is a tussock-dotted clearing, mainly red and silver tussock and a selection of grasses. Forest is unable to establish on the old river gravels, as cold spots and periodic flooding prevent seedling development.

From just before the hut a 40-minute return detour is signposted to Iris Burn Falls. These impressive 15 m falls disgorge the contents of the Iris Burn River over a rock bluff hemmed in by a cleft in the rock. The rushing water has scooped out a large plunge pool in the softer rock below. A motley collection of rocks lines the banks, suitable seats from which to admire the cascade and receive a cooling of fine spray.

DAY THREE

The short hill downstream from the Iris Burn Hut is known to DoC staff as 'the grunter', as after the hut wardens walk in with eight days of food on their backs they are left a little breathless. The hill is a moraine left by the glacier as it retreated up the Iris Burn Valley.

Iris Burn Hut to Rocky Point
2¼ hours ▪ 8.5 km

After about 30 minutes passing through tall silver beech forest, the track opens to a clearing created by the Big Slip in 1984. Aptly named, this huge landslide followed a good old Fiordland dump of rain in January 1984, when nearly 600 mm of rain fell on the tops in 24 hours. The volume of water sliding down the hillside was enough to create a slip plane below the shallow-rooting forest trees clinging to the treacherously steep hillside and the thin soils. Forest and all tumbled down leaving an impressive slip face and an estimated 300,000 m³ of debris fanned out across the valley floor. Big Slip is the most recent in a series of slips down the steep-sided valley.

A typical succession of revegetation may first display wineberry, lowland ribbonwood, tree fuchsia, round-leaved coprosma and tutu colonising the bare slopes. Tutu, like gorse and manuka, is an important nitrogen fixer, enabling embryonic soils to develop.

Further moraines intermingle with forest notable for the sparse understorey, save a few crown ferns, mosses and mingimingi. In the clearings, the hookgrass along the trackside can act as something of a brake in autumn, when the prolific crook-shaped seeds attach themselves to hairs and socks. Shave your legs or wear gaiters. These grasses have evolved to have seeds that attach to the feathers of flightless birds such as the kiwi and kakapo, as a means of dispersal. It is one of nature's beautiful partnerships.

On the way to the toilet, small clearing and DoC work hut at Rocky Point, look for golf ball fungus and orchids. The golf ball fungus also has a partnership with the beech trees in Chile, suggesting an association going back to Gondwanaland days.

BACK FROM THE BRINK

The takahe, the largest rail in the world, happily scratched a living in New Zealand for thousands of years until the arrival of the first humans. With Polynesian and European settlers, however, came predators and competition for food sources, and the annihilation of the flightless bird was rapid. In 1948, when naturalist Dr Geoffrey Orbell descended from the Murchison Mountains with stories of a possible sighting of *Notornis mantelli*, he was received with incredulity – the last sighting had been 50 years earlier and the bird was presumed extinct. In a later foray, however, he captured a takahe. Measures were immediately put in place to preserve the remnant population of South Island takahe and the birds were reclassified as *Porphyrio mantelli hochstetteri*. Had Orbell not rediscovered the takahe when he did, the species would almost certainly now be extinct.

The takahe's main enemies are deer, which compete for the snow tussock, and stoats, which prey on chicks. Deer were drastically culled in the 1970s, when they were shot from helicopters, but this practice is now uneconomic and keeping numbers down is now an exercise in population minimisation rather than eradication. Stoats are controlled with trap lines on the mountainsides.

In November each year DoC's takahe team visits breeding territories, locating nests and holding a light source to the eggs to determine their fertility. Infertile eggs are removed to ensure

From Rocky Point the track begins its second short climb of the day – this one named Heartbreak Hill by DoC staff on account of the short steep climb required to get around a slip on the track. You are climbing onto a terrace of glacial outwash gravels deposited by meltwater streams.

Rocky Point to Moturau Hut
2 hours ■ 8 km

The Iris Burn is undercutting the soft mud, silt and sandstones at the base of the valley and active erosion on the bend is causing further slumping of the valley walls. Slip faces are occasionally visible through delicate beech foliage. Look for whio and yellowheads on this section of the track.

On a few occasions the track drops down into a stream. From these viewpoints a few metres above the surroundings, the carpet of crown ferns smothering the forest floor is striking. Among them are kiokio, with pointed fronds, and the diminutive black hard fern, with occasional purple fronds.

As you approach the mouth of the Iris Burn (30 minutes before Moturau Hut), there's a short detour to the river, where you can see Lake Manapouri for the first time. The track traces a path over the delta built up by the river as it reaches the lake. Rivers transport sand and silt downstream, before depositing them when they reach a barrier such as a lake. As the sediment drops, it raises the bed of the lake – hence Shallow Bay, beside which sits the hut.

takahe expend their full efforts on eggs that are likely to hatch. If a nest has two fertile eggs, one is flown by helicopter in a portable incubator to Burwood, a rearing facility near Te Anau, where it is cared for until hatching.

Young chicks are fed using puppet heads that resemble their natural parents, and recorded bird calls are played to them. Foster parents also teach the young how to find the *Hypolepis millefolium* fern, an important component of the winter diet. At the end of September, Burwood chicks are released into the wild.

Some of these chicks wear transmitters. These are worn as backpacks with a piece of wetsuit rubber glued on to provide extra insulation in winter. The transmitter signals, which can be detected up to 10 km away, have dramatically increased the ease with which DoC staff can capture birds to study them. Trained dogs are the only other means of efficiently locating birds.

DoC's efforts have been rewarded with a total population approaching 200 birds in Fiordland in highly managed sanctuaries in the Murchison and Stewart Mountains, and a further 100 birds on predator-free offshore islands. The takahe is one of New Zealand's success stories in rescuing a species from the edge of extinction.

There are teasing glimpses of the lake through the forest edge and the golden sand at the edge of the lake seems impossibly bright in the full sun. Mt Titiroa, with its exposed granite top, also reflects the sun, with such intensity it sometimes looks like there is snow cover when there is not. Rona Island is visible in the lake and, as you reach Moturau Hut, Beehive and Pomona Islands also come to view. These outcrops scoured by advancing glaciers display the classic *roche moutonnée* form of one smooth, gently sloping side and one steeper, more jagged side.

Moturau Hut (185 m) is in a small clearing on the shore of Lake Manapouri. The 40-bunk hut looks down West Arm of Lake Manapouri to foreboding peaks such as Steep Peak and Leaning Peak. The Cathedral Peaks guard the western skyline. Toilets and picnic benches are provided for three-day trampers, who must continue to Rainbow Reach before the day is out. Display panels in the hut show an early map produced by surveyor James McKerrow, who named the Kepler Mountains, Murchison Mountains and Iris Burn. A brief examination of the dastardly sandfly is also posted along with DoC photos of the track and hut construction.

DAY FOUR

Moturau Hut to Rainbow Reach
1¾ hours ▪ 6 km

About 20 minutes on from the hut, Shallow Bay Hut is signposted to the right. This 30-minute detour, not included in the walking time for this section, heads for the beach. On the left a display panel names prominent mountains and islands on the far side of the lake. The track dives into the forest behind the lake before arriving at a good old-fashioned six-bunk Kiwi back-country hut. Retrace your steps to get back to the main track.

The track undulates through lowland beech forest with occasional rimu, matai and Hall's totara. Kahikatea also enjoy having wet feet beside occasional bogs, the most impressive of which, Amoeboid Mire, is crossed on a boardwalk. After a brief section over another forested moraine ridge, a short detour along another boardwalk leads to a lookout and interpretation panels by the small lake.

Bogs such as this form in poorly drained hollows in the moraine. They act as giant sponges, drawing in water in times of flood, then releasing it slowly in times of drought. European pioneers saw bogs, marshes and swamps as stinking holes, and completely unproductive. One of their first actions was to drain as many wetland areas as possible. It is fortunate some such as Amoeboid Mire remain.

The sun orchid, with its deep blue petals that open only when the sun is out, grows on beds of sphagnum moss. Red sundews also add splashes of colour. These small red plants look harmless and they are – unless you happen to be a small insect attracted by the sweet scent and spray of red sepals, which are cunningly coated in a gelatinous adhesive. The poor insects become trapped and are slowly ingested by these carnivorous beauties. Other notable cushion plants include the comb sedge and the moss-like *Centrolepis ciliata*.

The more than 200 plant species recorded in these bogs provide habitat for birds, fish and invertebrates. Scaups swim on the waters, fernbirds scurry around the rushes, and dragonflies and grasshoppers make forays around the fertile habitats. Celery pine and bog pine form occasional shrubs in the flats with *Dracophyllum oliveri*, wiwi and wire rush. A look behind the lookout platform reveals the forest succession from sphagnum moss through tall rushes to celery pine and bog pine on the fringes.

This entire section of track from the mouth of the Iris Burn past Rainbow Reach to the control gates is on the huge terminal moraine that separates Lakes Te Anau and Manapouri. The upper course of the Waiau River has crossed the moraine as it flows from Lake Te Anau to Lake Manapouri. Rivers rarely flow straight, and the upper Waiau is no exception. Cutting a sinuous course through the terminal moraine, the river performs a series of large looping curves, one of which, Balloon Loop, is to the right of the track. Most likely this will soon be cut off to form an oxbow lake.

Views downstream along the Waiau lead to the mountains south of Lake Manapouri, often mystically shadowed in cloud and always stately and grandiose. Soon after the track reaches the long, large footbridge spanning the Waiau to Rainbow Reach, an entry/exit point of the track for the three-dayers. This bridge was constructed as part of the Manapouri Power Scheme and opened on 11 September 1976. The erosion of the banks was a result of uncontrolled discharge from Lake Te Anau. These discharges have now been legislated against.

A cross-section of a river's current reveals a line of fastest flowing water that weaves from one outside bank to the other. This is known as the thalweg. Fast-flowing water has the potential for greater erosion and gnaws away at the outside of the curve, while the slow-flowing water drops material on the inside, exaggerating the curve. Eventually the bend may become horseshoe-shaped, with only a narrow neck of land between the banks. In time the river bursts through the neck, stranding the former course as an oxbow lake.

Rainbow Reach to control gates
3 hours ■ 9.5 km

This final section of the track passes through predominantly mountain beech and silver beech forest, with the occasional red beech on drier sites. Look for the rounded riverstone banks as the track climbs to traverse old river terraces, an indication of the height of the Waiau River when it was draining the vast ice sheets of the Fiordland mountains. Occasional clearings now cloaked with sooty mould covered manuka were once used by pioneer Jack Beer.

As you walk, much of the time you will be within earshot of the rippling waters of the Waiau River. The river views become more expansive closer to the control gates.

Control gates to Te Anau
50 min ■ 3 km

Retrace your early steps through the wildlife centre to Te Anau and your accommodation. It's a pleasing way to end the walk, to return to where you began.

TUATAPERE HUMP RIDGE TRACK

RIGHT: The Edwin Burn viaduct is a legacy of the sawmilling days at Port Craig. Industrious community efforts have raised the money needed to keep them safe, although in Waitutu's wet climes this is an ongoing process.

BELOW: A cheeky kea says 'good morning' to a Hump Ridge sunrise. This kea and his mates had fun sliding down the Okaka Hut roof at daybreak.

OVERLEAF: The sandstone tors and rippling tarns of the Hump Ridge give the landscape an other-worldly feel. These resistant outcrops have been etched by the fury of wind and rain, and moulded to contorted shapes and bizarre forms.

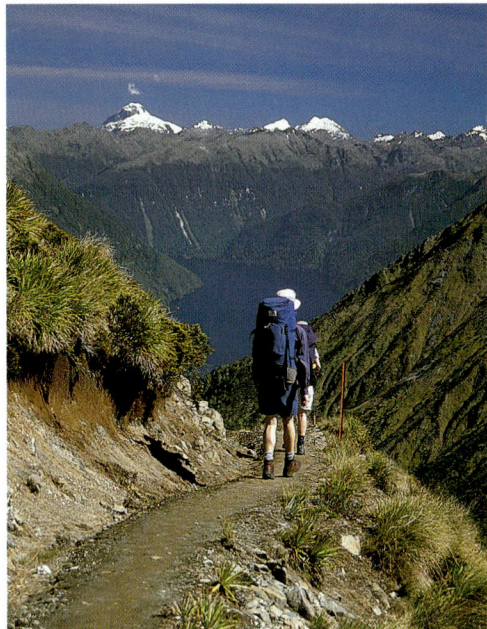

KEPLER TRACK

ABOVE LEFT: Moss and lichen in the perfect alpine gardens. ABOVE RIGHT: Day two on the Kepler is almost entirely on the tops. BELOW: Walking a steep-sided arête between two watersheds. OPPOSITE TOP: Luxmore Hut has breathtaking views across Lake Te Anau. OPPOSITE BOTTOM: The walk out along the Iris Burn Valley.

MILFORD TRACK

OPPOSITE TOP LEFT: The temperate rainforest in the Arthur Valley drips with mosses, lichens and epiphytes.
OPPOSITE TOP RIGHT: The memorial to Quintin McKinnon. OPPOSITE BOTTOM: Trampers above the '12 second drop'
look down the Arthur Valley. ABOVE: Sutherland Falls (580 m), once thought to be the highest in the world.

HOLLYFORD TRACK

ABOVE: The Darran Mountains, seen here from the Pyke River swingbridge, are the highest range in Fiordland. The granite peaks rising abruptly from the valley floor are a mecca for experienced mountaineers.

LEFT: The Hollyford Valley features many small trackside streams.

LEFT: On clear days the waters of the Hollyford River look almost tropical.

ABOVE: Fiordland crested penguins breed at Long Reef until early December.

BELOW: The 8 km Martins Bay spit, with pingao prominent on the ridge crests, is one of the least modified dune systems in the country.

ROUTEBURN TRACK

ABOVE: Key Summit has a 360-degree view, here looking towards Lake Marian. Early runholders George Gunn and David McKellar first spied the Hollyford Valley from this point.

RIGHT: Time for a snooze by Lake Mackenzie Hut.

OPPOSITE TOP: Lake Mackenzie on a tranquil autumn day.

OPPOSITE BOTTOM: The Harris Saddle Shelter can be a lifesaver during ugly weather. This route was followed by early Maori on their journeys to find pounamu (greenstone). It was also the favoured line for the planned road from Queenstown to Jamestown.

GREENSTONE AND CAPLES TRACKS

ABOVE: McKellar Saddle, the highest point on the tramp, offers the best views of the Earl Mountains.
BELOW: The Caples River was named after Patrick Caples, who in 1863 became the first European to walk through the valley. OPPOSITE: Red *Trentepohlia* algae coat many boulders in the Caples Valley.

REES–DART TRACK

LEFT: The lower Rees Valley is a wide-open expanse of grassland with cattle grazing below the Earnslaw massif.

BELOW: The Dart Glacier is a mesmerising focal point for the walk to Cascade Saddle. Like most glaciers elsewhere in the world, it is currently retreating – it has been estimated to recede 3 m every year.

ABOVE: Tussocks beside the Rees River.

RIGHT: Mt Edward is the most prominent peak seen by trampers during their descent of Rees Saddle.

BELOW: Mt Aspiring, Mt Avalanche and Rob Roy Peak from Cascade Saddle. On a fine day it would be hard to beat this view. The hardest decision is where to look, as the Dart Glacier fills the view on the western side.

LEFT: The Mount Cook lily is the largest buttercup in the world. These unique alpine plants, with their huge bowl-shaped leaves, flower in late spring and early summer. You can expect to find them on the Rees–Dart and on upland sections of other tracks.

BELOW: Kea are constant companions above the treeline. Gregarious, intelligent and mischievous, these parrots are easy to befriend. But they have become lazy in their eating habits and go after junk food handouts from trampers. It's important to leave them to find their own food.

MILFORD TRACK

60 km ■ four days ■ one way ■ Great Walk

The Milford Track is undoubtedly the most famous tramp in New Zealand, an iconic trip into the heart of Fiordland that for some people is their main reason for a visit to these shores. Ask a would-be visitor to New Zealand to name a tramp here, and the answer would most likely be the Milford Track. Around 7000 freedom walkers a year travel the track, joined by the same number of guided walkers, following in the footsteps of those early explorers such as Quintin McKinnon. Although this showpiece tramp embodies all that makes Fiordland so special, it is a physical challenge with a crossing of Mackinnon Pass and rough track sections.

Day one is just a short introduction to the grand setting of the walk. Taking the boat trip up Lake Te Anau is like crossing the Rubicon into a different world – one of sheer peaks, gliding rivers and verdant rainforest. You begin to understand you're entering a place that is very special. On day two the emerald waters of the Clinton River, graced with whio, slide beside the track. The imposing polished granite walls of the Clinton Canyon hem in the valley, with waterfalls tumbling down their faces. Mackinnon Pass becomes visible and draws you up the valley to the night's accommodation, Mintaro Hut at the base of towering Mt Balloon.

Day three is the toughest, with a crossing of Mackinnon Pass. There's a climb of 600 m but the grunt brings you into the alpine zone. In clear weather the views down the Clinton and Arthur Valleys are mesmerising, but on a wet day this is not a place to hang around. The knee-jerking descent follows the Roaring Burn to a detour to Sutherland Falls. The 580 m waterfall is the fifth highest in the world and a truly humbling sight. The night is spent at nearby Dumpling Hut. The forests dripping with moss, high mountain peaks covered year round in snow and the Arthur River are highlights of day four, with views of Lake Ada to cap it all. The aptly named Sandfly Point is the terminus for the walk.

The Milford Track dates back well over a century to 1888, when Quintin McKinnon found a route up the Clinton Valley and over the pass that would later bear his name (albeit spelled differently), linking up with a tourist track to Sutherland Falls built by Milford identity Donald Sutherland. Early walkers were less than impressed with the quality of the new track, but more than impressed with their guide, Quintin McKinnon. Sutherland had already built Beech Hut near the falls, but further huts were built in the Clinton Valley – McKinnon's hut opposite Neale Burn and Pompolona Camp. Conditions were rough, to put it mildly, but the track was up and running.

Despite McKinnon's untimely death in 1892 there were many who were eager to follow in his footsteps and walk the track. Less adventurous visitors would cruise into Milford and spend a night at Beech Hut before viewing the Sutherland Falls. The scenery won many over and before long word was out. The Milford was something special. The government, keen to attract wealthy tourists, invested in track building and infrastructure, sometimes employing prison gangs and private contractors to upgrade the trail. The palatial Glade House, financed by Te Anau Downs station owner Edward Melland, and run by John and Louisa Garvey, rapidly acquired a reputation for conviviality.

In 1903 the Tourist Department bought Glade House and the track, setting to work on marketing the whole deal. They struck it lucky when they invited Blanche Baughan, a New Zealand poet, to walk the track in 1908. She wrote an article for the London *Spectator* that she titled 'A Notable Walk', later embellished by an editor to become 'The Finest Walk in the World'. This well-used catchphrase has done much for the tramp's recognition around the globe and also for New Zealand's promotion from the status of backwater to tourist destination.

At this time walkers were treated to a salubrious welcome at the Milford end by Elizabeth Sutherland, wife of the man who cut that first track to Sutherland Falls. Weary travellers were nourished with such delights as curried crayfish. Following Donald's death in 1919, Elizabeth bowed out of her hospitality role. The Milford Hotel was constructed in 1928 and the track was upgraded with bridges over the Arthur River and newer huts along the track, including a shelter at Mackinnon Pass.

By the 1960s members of the Otago Tramping Club were becoming increasingly disgruntled at the fact only paying guided walkers could sample the Milford Track's delights. Why should one of New Zealand's most celebrated attractions be the domain of just a few? They set out to prove the track could be walked independently, and despite battling floods, they succeeded in establishing the right of 'freedom walkers' to

SECTION TIMINGS

DAY ONE 1½ hours 5 km

Glade wharf to Clinton Hut	1½ hours	5 km

DAY TWO 6 hours 17 km

Clinton Hut to Hirere Shelter	1¾ hours	7 km
Hirere Shelter to Bus Stop Shelter	2 hours	5 km
Bus Stop Shelter to Mintaro Hut	2¼ hours	5 km

DAY THREE 8 hours 19.5 km

Mintaro Hut to Mackinnon Pass	2¼ hours	5 km
Mackinnon Pass to Quintin Lodge	2½ hours	7.5 km
Sutherland Falls (optional)	1½ hours	4 km return
Quintin Lodge to Dumpling Hut	1 hour	3 km

DAY FOUR 6 hours 18.5 km

Dumpling Hut to Boatshed	1½ hours	5.5 km
Boatshed to Giant Gate Shelter	2½ hours	7.5 km
Giant Gate Shelter to Sandfly Point	1½ hours	5.5 km

ply the route. In 1966 the Fiordland National Park Board erected huts at Clinton Forks, Lake Mintaro and Dumpling. Although modified in site and design, these huts are still used by the do-it-yourselfers today.

As you walk the track today, it is patently obvious you are literally following in the footsteps of many pioneering, determined and visionary people. All who have trodden the route, however, come away with one overriding impression, of a landscape beyond parallel.

BOOKING

As this is a DoC Great Walk, all huts (Clinton Hut 40 bunks, Mintaro Hut 40 bunks, Dumpling Hut 40 bunks) must be booked in advance. It is always booked months ahead, so if you want to be sure of a place, it's advisable to get on the DoC website (www.doc.govt.nz) as soon as possible after 1 July to book. Otherwise you will have to rely on a last-minute cancellation and may miss out altogether. There is no camping on the track, anywhere.

It is possible to walk the track with guides, staying in private lodges (www.ultimatehikes.co.nz).

Terralink's Milford & Kepler Tracks map is the best for this area. DoC's Milford Track Parkmap 335-01 is also available.

GETTING THERE

It is easiest to book a standard transport package to and from the track. All the details are outlined on the Milford Track independent walk application form (www.doc.govt.nz). The journey starts with a bus trip from Queenstown or Te Anau to Te Anau Downs. Next is a boat trip to Glade wharf and the start of the track. At the end of the walk, a boat will take you from Sandfly Point to Freshwater Basin at the head of Milford Sound, and a bus takes you back to Queenstown, Te Anau or another Great Walk. Some people like to add a cruise on Milford Sound at the end of their tramp.

Generally an itinerary would work like this. A bus ride takes you to Te

Anau Downs to catch the Real Journeys boat to Glade wharf at 10.30 am or 2 pm (20 available places per journey). At the other end, Red Boats runs the Sandfly Point service at 2 pm, with a further 10 places at 3.15 pm. The Tracknet bus then departs at either 2.30 pm to Te Anau or Queenstown, or 5 pm to Te Anau only.

DAY ONE

This is a fine piece of forest – lofty, dense and varied. The mountain beech and silver beech are both dwarfed by monolithic red beech, which give their presence away by the confetti of decaying red leaves on the track. Red beech are the dominant tree in the lower Clinton below Pompolona, before they give way to silver and mountain beech. An understorey of Hall's totara, horopito, lancewood and broadleaf form an impenetrable barrier of green, aided by a forest floor smothered in crown ferns and mosses of vibrant green. From late summer, keep an eye out for greenhood orchids and sensitise your nose to the sweet pungent smell of the New Zealand Easter orchid, one of our epiphytic orchids.

Glade wharf to Clinton Hut
1½ hours ▪ 5 km

Glade House is now rather roomier than the original construction and painted less garishly. It is still in a clearing encircled by steep rock walls and the Clinton River. Whio, with their characteristic 'whiiiiiiiiooooooooo' call, dabble in the green waters of the Clinton and perch proudly on the banks.

Glade House's beginnings came in 1895 when John and Louisa Garvey fell in love with the spot and determined to build a house there. The wealthy landowners of Te Anau Downs station stumped up the cash for construction and by the 1895–96 walking season the long verandah was awash with roses. After their arduous voyage up the lake, track walkers were greeted in sumptuous surroundings. The Garveys and their 11 children maintained a reputation for lavish hospitality until their departure in 1908. After the government bought the Milford Track in 1903 the house was extended, but in 1929 the entire building was burnt to a cinder. It was later reconstructed, and today Glade House is an overnight stop for guided walkers.

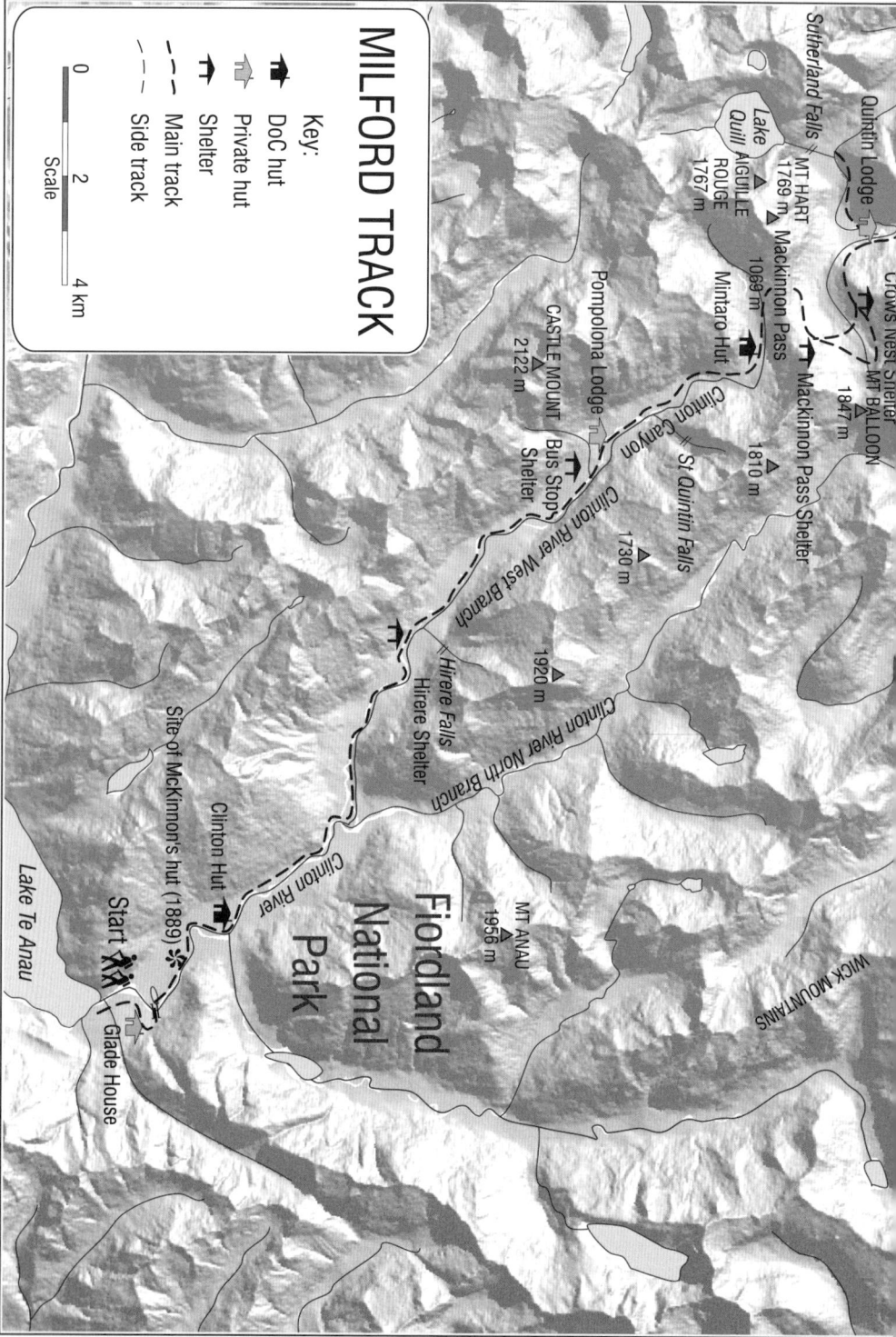

MILFORD TRACK

Key:

⬛➡ DoC hut
⬜➡ Private hut
⬛➡ Shelter
– – – Main track
— — Side track

Scale
0   2   4 km

Sutherland Falls

Quintin Lodge

Lake Quill

MT HART 1769 m

AIGUILLE ROUGE 1767 m

Mackinnon Pass 1069 m

Crows Nest Shelter

MT BALLOON 1847 m

Mintaro Hut

Mackinnon Pass Shelter

1810 m

Pompolona Lodge

CASTLE MOUNT 2122 m

Bus Stop Shelter

Clinton River West Branch

Clinton Canyon

St Quintin Falls

1730 m

1920 m

Clinton River North Branch

Hirere Falls

Hirere Shelter

MT ANAU 1956 m

WICK MOUNTAINS

Site of McKinnon's hut (1889)

Clinton Hut

Clinton River

Fiordland National Park

Lake Te Anau

Start

Glade House

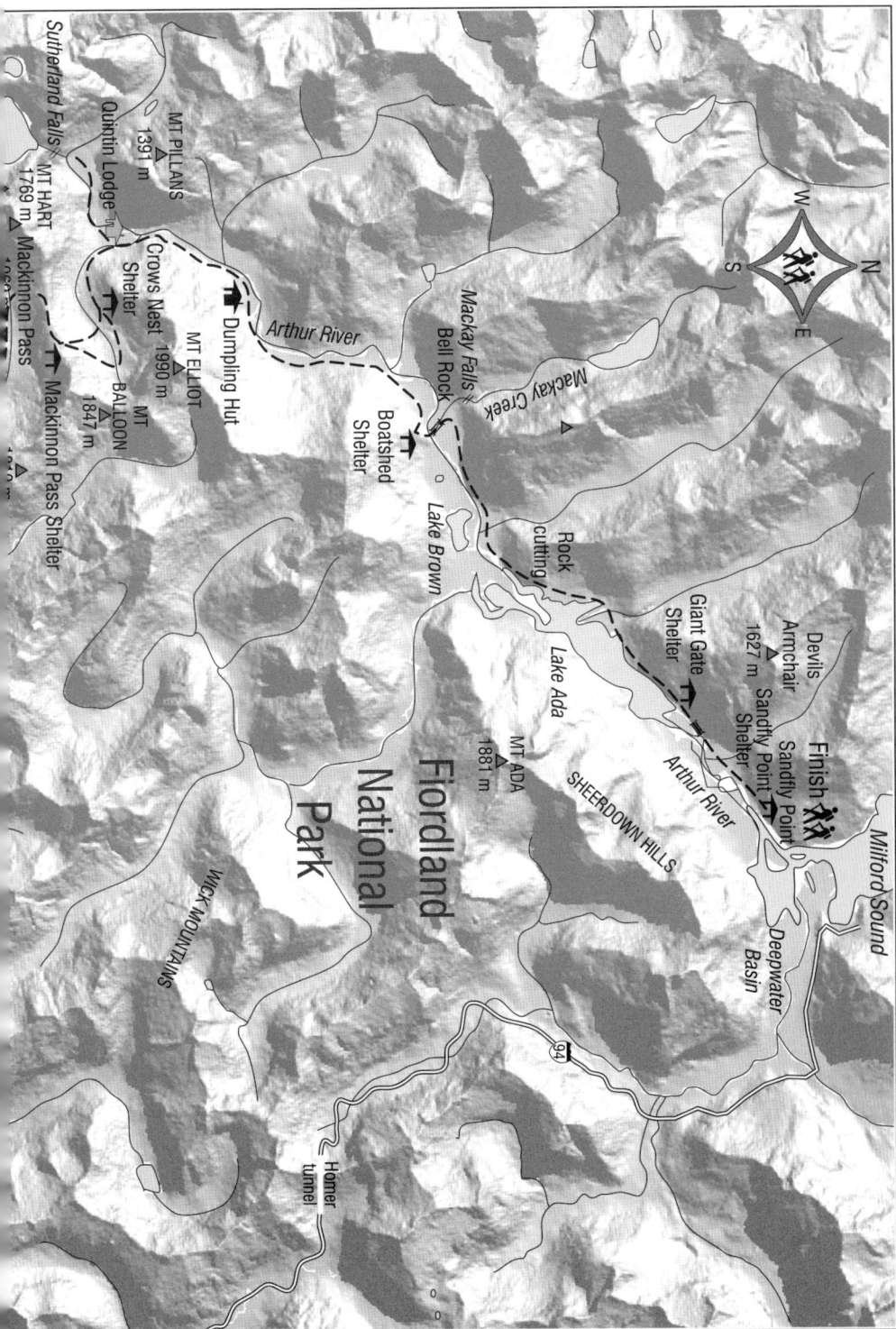

Sutherland Falls

MT HART
1769 m

Mackinnon Pass

Mackinnon Pass Shelter

Quintin Lodge

MT PILLANS
1391 m

Crows Nest
Shelter

MT ELLIOT

MT
BALLOON
1847 m

Dumpling Hut

Arthur River

Mackay Falls
Bell Rock

Mackay Creek

Boatshed
Shelter

Lake Brown

Rock
cutting

Lake Ada

MT ADA
1881 m

SHEERDOWN HILLS

Giant Gate
Shelter

Arthur River

Devils
Armchair

Sandfly Point
Shelter

Sandfly Point

1627 m

Deepwater
Basin

Milford Sound

Finish

WICK MOUNTAINS

Fiordland
National
Park

94

Homer
tunnel

N
W   E
S

Until the first swingbridge was built, walkers were rowed across the Clinton River to continue their journey. Three swingbridges were washed away until this final 1978 version acted on the lessons learned. The wide track now follows the river and was once used by a tractor and trailer to ferry supplies to the huts further up the valley. The sandy base of the river seems to illuminate the water from below, and with its deep turquoise colour the river resembles a tropical lagoon. Its wide course and smooth surface are only broken by the punctuation of raindrops or the wake of a whio.

Go past the sign for Quintin McKinnon's first hut, opposite the Neale Burn, with its majestic view up the large valley. The building was built on piles to avoid the floods and furnished with bunks. It fell into disrepair following the construction of Glade House.

Shortly after a bend in the river with a view up to Dore Pass, a detour to a wetland walk is signposted (15 minutes return). The final sections are boardwalked to keep your feet dry and more importantly to protect the fragile sphagnum bogs underfoot. Interpretation panels explain the ecology of the wetland and its importance in the stages of forest succession. The sphagnum is joined in this wetland by sundews and sedges. Near the transition zone at the forest/wetland margin are celery pine, bog pine and turpentine. The lack of forest cover here allows fine views up the Clinton Valley North Branch.

Soon after the wetland, Clinton Hut is signposted to the left.

> Sphagnum is a celebrated New Zealand bog plant that can hold up to 20 times its volume of water. Growers of exotic flowers overseas find it useful to keep roots moist during transportation.

DAY TWO

Clinton Hut to Hirere Shelter
1¾ hours ■ 7 km

The luxuriant forest continues all the way from the Clinton Hut to the Clinton Forks, where the North Branch of the Clinton River meets the West Branch. The hut that used to be here was washed away in yet another flood, but the toilet still stands. Lofty red beech mingle with silver beech and no colour but green is visible in the forest interior.

On the left 45 minutes after Clinton Forks, a large slip that tumbled down in 1982 is a graphic reminder of the volatile landscape. The mass of material slid inexorably over the valley floor, diverting the river and damming a small lake from which ghostly stumps protrude today. *Stereocaulon corticatulum* lichen colonises the bare rocks, making the first steps in the evolution back to forest. There used be an old hut called Six Mile Hut near here but, although it survived the slip, it was removed for fear of a later avalanche finishing off the job.

If it is raining heavily, the next section (40 minutes) to Hirere Falls will likely be a rude introduction to wading. The marker poles raised above the track hint to those on a drier trip how high the water can reach. The Hirere Shelter is for guided walkers but has a toilet all can use.

Hirere Shelter to Bus Stop Shelter
2 hours ■ 5 km

The Maori name Hirere means 'waterfall' and on the next section of track, when you are out of the forest, the reason for this naming is obvious – in wet weather the imposing granite wall opposite is threaded with waterfalls, the most permanent of which is Hirere Falls.

The first view of Mackinnon Pass appears as a low point dwarfed by the surrounding peaks. Mintaro Hut, your destination for today, is at the base of the pass. A short detour winds around to Hidden Lake, the receptacle for the waterfalls gushing off the mountainside. In late summer, after the threat of avalanches has receded, this is a good swimming hole. Prairie Lake, a little further on, is another good place for a swim.

The shrubby vegetation on these clearer sections of valley floor is all that is allowed by the frequent avalanches that sweep off the mountains. The regeneration is dominated by tree fuchsia, with its glowing orange trunks and pink flowers in spring. In colder districts and in high country it is deciduous in winter. Mountain holly, hebes, wineberry, mountain ribbonwood and Maori onion are found here.

A gentle climb takes you out of the flat glacial valley bottom to the shelter at Marlenes Creek. In heavy rain the creek becomes a torrent. To avoid drowning, if the stream is high wait it out at the Bus Stop. Because of the steep watersheds in Fiordland, when the rain falls the creeks quickly rise. But when the rain stops you don't have to wait long for the water levels to drop. At the Bus Stop, talk with the kea but don't feed them.

Bus Stop Shelter to Mintaro Hut
2¼ hours ■ 5 km

When it's safe to cross Marlenes Creek, look for the white 'T' nailed to a silver beech to find the track on the far side. There's a toilet nearby and Pompolona Lodge, the second night for guided walkers, is a little further on. The first accommodation to replace McKinnon's rudimentary lodgings was built here in 1906 but was demolished by successive avalanches. It was rebuilt and enlarged several times to become the relative palace of today. Pompolona is named after the famous pompolonas Quintin McKinnon used to bake for his parties. These loosely resembled scones and were fried in mutton fat.

The track climbs and crosses a swingbridge. To the right, St Quintin Falls, which drop over 200 m, are visible. They were named by explorer (and future prime minister) Thomas Mackenzie in honour of the illustrious McKinnon, who had guided him over the pass. Mackenzie must have been indeed grateful to elevate McKinnon to sainthood! The forested spur ahead is the final feature you must traverse before you come to Mintaro Hut, 600 m above sea level. The rampart of Mt Balloon rises nearly 1700 m above.

If you have spare energy or the weather forecast is looking dodgy for tomorrow, the evening is a good time to head up to the pass. It is generally less populated than it is during the day and the light is sublime.

DAY THREE

Mintaro Hut to Mackinnon Pass
2¼ hours ■ 5 km

Wake up, rise and climb! There is a 554 m ascent to the pass awaiting you. The key is to take it slowly and not allow yourself to become breathless – you should be able to conduct a conversation while walking. Better to be a tortoise than a hare – find a rhythm and don't stop too often to admire the view.

Beautiful Lake Mintaro, close to the hut, was called Lake Beautiful before it took on the name of Fred Mintaro Muir, an early photographer who navigated the track. To Maori it was known as Te Hapuawhio (whio lagoon). Views of the lake and how it is positioned at the head of the receding Clinton Canyon become more acute as you begin your climb.

It's around 5 km to the top, the track snaking around 11 hairpins. There are views down the Clinton Canyon and the surrounding towers of Mt Hart (1769 m), Aiguille Rouge (1767 m) and the conspicuous peak of Mt Balloon (1847 m), named by Donald Sutherland in 1880 as it was 'sticking up out of the mist like a balloon'.

As the forest dwindles to tussock after the sixth zigzag, you are truly in the alpine domain, with its delicate displays of flowers most enticing in early summer. Look out for the conspicuous Mount Cook lily, with its large leaves and bold white flowers. Other notable plants are whipcord hebes, snow marguerites, eyebright, mountain daisies and pineapple scrub. The tussock is mainly mid-ribbed snow tussock.

As the gradient diminishes, your gaze will be captured by the cross atop a stone cairn erected by the Gaelic Society, Otago Rugby Football Union and the government as a memorial to Quintin McKinnon. On a clear day the views from the col are stupendous. Following the view around from Mt Hart to your left, the first major peak is Mt Mackenzie (1592 m) above Lake Quill, the source of Sutherland Falls. On the far side of Staircase Creek is Mt Pillans (1391 m), dwarfing Quintin Lodge and the airstrip on the valley floor. Leading behind Quintin is the Green Valley, headed by the Lady of the Snows (1818 m), a majestic peak you will get to know over the rest of the walk. The retreat of the Arthur Valley is hidden behind spurs, but the nearby Jervois Glacier, the final remnant of the Arthur Valley's excavating glacier, is perched below Mt Elliot (1926 m). Mt Balloon (1846 m) closes the northern view to the right. Behind you is the Clinton Canyon and its sentry line of pyramidal peaks. This is the last you'll see of the valley. Don't step too close to the edge here – the cliff is known all too vividly as the '12-second drop'.

On a bad day the view will be confined to your imagination. When the weather is particularly unpleasant, which is not uncommon at this very exposed spot, you may need to cower low in defiance of the wind and hold on to snow tussock for support. Visibility may be less than 10 m and however tight you pull the drawcord of your hood, the sleet may prick your cheeks like a pincushion and your eyelids will burn with the cold. It may be that all you will hear is the splashing of rain off your hood and your internal voice asking 'Why am I doing this?' You will understand why to Maori the pass was known as Omanui (place to move over quickly).

On these days, Mackinnon Pass Shelter at the high point of the track (1146 m) is a life-saver. The hut is the fifth on this site, the rest having been blown away by hurricane-force winds. This particular incarnation has meaty steel bolts embedded in the concrete pad, shackled to cables anchoring the roof trusses. There are also kea, pipits and rock wrens – and the 'loo with the view' of Clinton Canyon. Look for rock sheep plants hugging the rocks in an attempt to conserve moisture.

Mackinnon Pass to Quintin Lodge
2½ hours ■ 7.5 km

The descent from the col is very exposed and in inclement conditions brings more hardship. The lengthy downward march requires concentration and careful positioning of each footfall, and is tough on the knees. The imposing cliffs of Mt Elliot rise beside the track as it weaves through areas colonised by Fiordland speargrass, mountain flax and more Mount Cook lilies. At a gate you will be directed either around the main track (loosely following the perimeter of the bowl) or on the alternative emergency track. This route, hand hewn by legendary 'trackie' Bill Anderson, goes straight down the hillside and is used if there is avalanche danger. It exits just below the Crows Nest Shelter, a tea stop for guided walkers.

On the main track a sign points out a view of the top tier of Sutherland Falls, before the track crosses a bridge over Moraine Creek. Roaring Burn is flanked by welcome staircases and boardwalks. Be sure to occasionally look behind at the waterfalls framed elegantly by silver beech branches. The granite is worn smooth and etched with the flowlines of passing floods.

The descent continues past sprays of Prince of Wales ferns. The sight and sound of more waterfalls fill your eyes and ears. Dudleigh Falls is a neat fall into a circular hollow, while Lyndsay Falls jettisons over a bluff in the river bed. In heavy rain this track section becomes a creek. Keep glancing up and you can see the source of your soaking hundreds of metres above. The walls of water are impressive as they race to the sea in cascades, streams and rivers.

If you plan to take the side trip to Sutherland Falls, follow the sign to Quintin.

Sutherland Falls
1½ hours ■ 4 km return

Although your knees are probably wobbling like jelly and the thought of walking an extra 4 km may not be too enticing, the side trip to Sutherland Falls is a must. Leave your pack at the public day shelter at Quintin Lodge.

The track to the falls passes through tree fuchsia forest and is studded with hen and chicken fern and hound's tongue fern. The moisture loving ferns are taking advantage of the frequent sprays of water from the Sutherland Falls.

When you are 580 m from the base of the falls, a sign indicates that you are now the same distance away from the falls as they are tall. The leaps appear in sequence, 248 m the first, 229 m the second and 103 m the final drop. The decibels increase as you get closer to the roaring base, where thousands of tonnes of water reach the conclusion of their descent from Lake Quill. It is a truly humbling experience witnessing this show of aquatic fireworks.

The descent from Quintin is known as the Gentle Annie Hill and has been the subject of experimentation by DoC, with track workers adding concrete splatters to hinder the perpetual washing away of track metal. This section has been nicknamed 'Cowpat Alley'. Below the Quintin footbridge, as the track skirts the Arthur River, there is an impressive view up to Sutherland Falls, and clearings further down allow views to Dumpling Hill and another peek at the Lady of the Snows. The track crosses Sandy Flat, another area cleared by avalanches, then follows a gantry bolted to the rock face. Dumpling Hut is on the right.

Quintin Lodge to Dumpling Hut
1 hour ■ 3 km

DAY FOUR

The long straights of the track below Dumpling Hut are known as 'the race course'. From the 1930s, when packhorses were used to cart supplies to the huts, this track section was the only place they got a run out. Some of the slips take their names from notable packhorses.

Dumpling Hut to Boatshed
1½ hours ■ 5.5 km

The forest composition is different now that you are on the west coast. The warmer and wetter microclimate is reflected in the greater density of growth and the presence of new species such as rata. Ferns are more prolific, including tree ferns such as the rough tree fern.

The track crosses the newest (December 2003) and ugliest of all the slips on the walk. Any bowled beech you encounter in Fiordland's forests exhibit the root plate, demonstrating the shallow rooting system of the trees. Rather than attempt a penetration below the shallow soils, the trees have radial root systems that intertwine with neighbouring trees – they literally hold each other up. All it takes is for one tree to lose hold, usually when heavy rains have created a slip plane below the soil, and the whole forest comes tumbling down.

There's a toilet just before the Boatshed, a historic building now used by guided walkers. Early walkers had to cross the Arthur River here in a rather undignified way, in a cage suspended under a cable. This was replaced in 1909 by a light suspension bridge that was washed away during the next flood. It was replaced in 1910 and a year later this structure also failed. For six decades a boat service was used, and the slipway, winch and diminutive corrugated iron sheds that remain hark back to the more rustic days of track walking. Another bridge was erected in 1972 and today's bridge is the latest span over the river. During a good flood, water can still flow to just below the treads.

Boatshed to Giant Gate Shelter
2½ hours ■ 7.5 km

On the northern bank of the Arthur River the track uses a boardwalk to save traipsing through the swamp. The rush of Mackay Falls becomes audible, turning to a loud roar as you climb the viewing platform. Named after Sutherland's exploring companion John Mackay, the falls are whipped into plumes of spray by the boulder-strewn creek. To Maori they were known as Te Huka-a-Tawhi (the foam of Tawhi).

The other feature of interest here is Bell Rock, so named because if you crawl underneath it the worn-out hollow resembles a bell. Take your torch and admire the rock-sculpted etchings and smooth curves. Bell Rock was formerly submerged in the creek and the relentless action of water-driven erosion ground the cavity to the impressive dimensions above you. A later flood or earth tremor then caused a rock fall and moved the rock to its current resting place.

Steep Hill now rises to the north and the track crosses the detritus from a series of slips. Some were dislodged by earthquakes, others by tree avalanches. One of these slips around 900 years ago blocked the Arthur River and Lake Ada filled up behind the natural dam. Near Lake Brown you may be glad of the elevated marker posts that guide the way – this is one of the most infamous flood sections on the track and the water can get to waist deep. The rainfall here is higher than on the other side of the pass and the lower altitude means warmer temperatures. Podocarps such as miro and rimu tower above the canopy of kamahi, broadleaf and tree ferns.

When you cross a couple more footbridges over Poseidon Creek look for the monster Donald Sutherland believed lived in the waterways. Such is the imagination of a hermit! The track skirts the lake in a cutting completed by prison gangs and contract workers in 1898. This is hard rock and it must have taken hard men to carry tools and supplies in loads approaching 30 kg from Sandfly Point. If you examine the excavations

PIONEERS OF MILFORD

Donald Sutherland, known as the hermit of Milford Sound, was a Scotsman by birth. He fought in the New Zealand Wars and in late 1877 sailed up Milford Sound in his small vessel *Porpoise* with his dog, Joe. This was the start of a long residence in the sound and the construction of the 'city of Milford'. His own residence, the Esperance Chalet, was a slab hut with a thatched roof, like the other buildings in the conurbation.

Sutherland's prime motive for settling at Milford was gold. But he found other excuses to explore. With John Mackay, a prospector from Big Bay, he ventured up adjoining valleys looking for a route from Queenstown to Milford Sound. In November 1880 they rowed up Lake Ada in the Arthur Valley and encountered a large waterfall, tossing a coin to see who would be immortalised in the naming. Mackay won the right to name Mackay Falls. Imagine his dismay when they found another, much bigger waterfall. In their initial excitement the explorers estimated Sutherland Falls to be 5700 feet (1737 m) high, although the true height is 1904 feet (580 m).

When word of the new discovery got out, early tourists made a beeline for the area. Sutherland was commissioned to blaze a trail to the cascade and build a slab hut, a replica of which now stands as Beech Hut. Cruise ships arrived with hordes of visitors and Sutherland soon became rather grumpy about the 'ashfelters' shattering his solitude with their incessant questioning.

Meanwhile, to the east of the Divide, a surveyor named Quintin McKinnon set off up the Clinton Valley with Ernest Mitchell. Their goal was to connect with the track to the falls, thereby establishing an overland route to Milford Sound. McKinnon and Mitchell spent several days living off the land, sampling such rare delights as kakapo, whio and kiwi. On 16 October 1888 they crossed the pass at the head of the Clinton Valley. The pass would become known as Mackinnon Pass, even though this is not the spelling McKinnon himself used. McKinnon and Mitchell continued down Roaring Burn to the Arthur Valley, eventually meeting up with Sutherland's track near the Beech Hut. McKinnon scribbled a note on a piece of paper and continued down the Arthur, only to meet up with a survey party headed by Charles Adams, chief surveyor of Otago. Together they ploughed on to Sutherland's 'city', mission accomplished.

closely you can still decipher the names of some track workers. Many 'smoko' breaks must have been spent chiselling signatures into the rock. If the liberal moss coverings were removed, there would likely be more examples of century-old graffiti.

There are good views from here of Lake Ada up the valley in the direction of Mt Kepka and opposite to the Sheerdown Peaks. You can also see up Joes River, named after Sutherland's dog. When the waters of Lake Ada are clear you can still make out tree stumps preserved in anaerobic conditions since the lake's formation. Descend to the lake once again and tune your ears to the sound of Giant Gate Falls.

Giant Gate Shelter to Sandfly Point
1½ hours ■ 5.5 km

Giant Gate Falls is a good spot for a break, either in the shelter watching the whio forage in the water or on the sunny rocks below the falls. The naming of the falls, again by Sutherland, seems apt as a large crevice frames the frothing flood, as if guarding the entry to another world.

The track passes a disused jetty, known as Doughboy, that was used as a staging post for supplies to service Quintin. In times gone by a tractor and trailer laden with goodies for tired walkers plied the wide track through open forest on the way to Sandfly Point. The sight of the shelter at Sandfly Point is a welcome sight. Grab the obligatory photo by the sign, now embellished with boots finished off by the Milford Track, then dash for cover in the sandfly-free zone of the shelter. According to Maori tradition, the mother of all sandflies was released here by Hine-nui-te-po. Her progeny swarm prolifically, ready to sap your final dregs of energy with the 'Milford wave'.

The boat ride to Freshwater Basin is a treat, and a fitting climax to your tramp.

HOLLYFORD TRACK

61 km ■ four days ■ one way

There can be few finer valleys in New Zealand than the Hollyford. From beginnings in the McPherson Glacier above Homer Saddle, the Hollyford River picks up momentum before diving north near the Marian Face and following its dramatic course to the sea. On its journey, the river captures the flow of many other watersheds, some emanating from the meltwaters of glaciers high in the Darrans. The Hollyford Track follows the valley floor virtually all the way to the coast. It's a journey from the mountains to the sea. Around 2000 trampers per year do the track, with another 700 or so on the guided walk. It is uncrowded for most of the year and one of the few tramps in Fiordland safe to attempt in winter.

On the first day most people aim to reach Lake Alabaster on the well-groomed surface. The 150 m climb over Little Homer Saddle is the most arduous ascent of the tramp. The forest is diverse and dense, the Hollyford River alluring. Hidden Falls tumble forcefully over a bluff, with the Darrans, capped by Mt Madeline and Mt Tutoko, rising on the far side of the valley. After you surmount Little Homer Saddle, Little Homer Falls is the next highlight, before you pass the Hollyford/Pyke confluence on the way to the first night's hut near Lake Alabaster.

Next day, misty swirls on the early morning lake are the parting memory as you cross the Pyke River and embark on the Demon Trail beside Lake McKerrow. The section to Demon Trail Hut is the roughest of any in this book and there are several creek crossings. Day three is more of the same, tackling three-wire bridges and undulating over rocky spurs to Hokuri Hut. The walkwires are not for anyone scared of heights – they involve balancing on a wire while holding two others at shoulder height.

On day four the track crosses the Alpine Fault at Hokuri Creek and follows the gravel lake shore to the site of Jamestown. The Podocarp Walk, with some fine examples of rimu trees, is a highlight before you come to the coast. The dune forest allows occasional glimpses of the Hollyford River and the Martins Bay spit, but the best views are saved for Martins Bay Hut. No journey down the Hollyford is complete without a trip to Long Reef to see the penguins (in season) and New Zealand fur seals.

The isolated Hollyford Valley has been the site of great human endeavours. Maori lived in the dunes behind Martins Bay until the 1860s, taking advantage of the abundant fish, eels, fowl and forest birds. They used the valley as a trading route on their journeys inland. Lake Alabaster was known as Wawahi-waka or 'to split wood for canoes'. A Maori settlement existed at Kotuku (Martins Bay) until the 1860s, when European explorations of the area commenced in earnest.

First on the scene, in 1863, was Patrick Quirk Caples, who ventured down the valley in search of gold and bestowed the European name of the valley. At the coast he spotted the huts of Kotuku, but as a lone traveller was too frightened to approach, fleeing back up the valley after ceremonially washing his hands in the sea to mark the first east–west crossing of Otago by a European.

Next in the flurry of visitors were Captain Alabaster and Malcolm 'Skipper' Duncan, who formed part of a prospecting party. They voyaged up Lake McKerrow in a cutter from the *Aquila* and made it eventually to Key Summit. On their return they rowed up to and named Lake Alabaster, overshadowed by the Skippers Range. No gold, so no interest in the area and off they sailed.

Enter geologist and explorer Dr James Hector, who navigated the treacherous Hollyford Bar and landed at Martins Bay. He found the Maori villagers Caples had been so frightened of were actually very welcoming.

SECTION TIMINGS

DAY ONE 6½ hours 19.5 km

Hollyford road end to Swamp Creek	1 hour	2 km
Swamp Creek to Hidden Falls Hut	2 hours	7 km
Hidden Falls Hut to Little Homer Falls	1½ hours	4 km
Little Homer Falls to Alabaster Hut	1¾ hours	6.5 km

DAY TWO 5 hours 14.5 km

Alabaster Hut to McKerrow Island	3 hours	9 km
McKerrow Island to Demon Trail Hut	2 hours	5.5 km

DAY THREE 6 hours 9.5 km

Demon Trail Hut to Hokuri Hut	6 hours	9.5 km

DAY FOUR 7 hours 17.5 km

Hokuri Hut to Podocarp Walk	2 hours	5.5 km
Podocarp Walk to Jerusalem Creek	1½ hours	4 km
Jerusalem Creek to Martins Bay Hut	1½ hours	4 km
Long Reef (optional)	2 hours	4 km return

Hector struck up a great friendship with Tutoko and renamed the chief's daughters Sara and May, names that are now remembered in the hills to the north and south of Martins Bay.

Hector's search for gold was in vain, but he returned to Queenstown with an idea to build a road down the Hollyford Valley to a new port on the west coast. The road was never built and the port, Jamestown, was abandoned within 10 years. A few Jamestown pioneers stayed behind, and the McKenzie family farmed the flat land behind the spit until they were bought out in 1926 by the legendary Davey Gunn.

In total Davey Gunn leased more than 10,000 hectares in the Hollyford, Pyke and Kaipo Valleys. His farming activities were later combined with taking tourists, sometimes on horseback, through the Hollyford and Pyke Valleys. These early trips were the precursor for today's tramp, which explores the rich natural and human histories the valley shadows.

BOOKING

As the Hollyford is not a Great Walk, huts cannot be booked. They are on a first-come first-served basis, but it will only be problem getting a bed during the December and January holidays. Hut tickets must be purchased in advance from DoC Te Anau or other DoC centres. Unlike Great Walks, gas is not supplied, so you will need your own stove. Huts are Hidden Falls Hut (12 bunks), Alabaster Hut (26 bunks), McKerrow Island Hut (12 bunks), Demon Trail Hut (12 bunks), Hokuri Hut (12 bunks) and Martins Bay Hut (12 bunks). Some huts are serviced during busy periods. Camping is permitted on the Hollyford, but not recommended as there are few places to pitch a tent, especially on the Demon Trail section.

Visit www.hollyfordtrack.com for details of the guided walk.

The Hollyford Track is covered by the NZ260 1:50,000 series maps D39 Lake McKerrow and D40 Milford.

GETTING THERE

The track starts at the end of Lower Hollyford Road. From Te Anau follow the Milford Road over the Divide. Lower Hollyford Road is signposted 5 km further on. Stop at Pops Lookout on the way to get a view down the Hollyford Valley. Better still go into the parking area higher up the hill where the views are less obscured. Next stop should be Gunns Camp. Started by Murray Gunn in the 1950s, this museum houses a motley selection of Fiordland memorabilia housed in salubrious surroundings. The displays give an insight into the history of the valley and region, but not without a sense of quirkiness.

The road end is 15.5 km from the junction with Milford Road. There's a parking area with a shelter near the start of the track.

Tracknet operates a daily service during the Great Walks season (end October to end April) to the end of the Lower Hollyford Road. Bookings are essential.

At the conclusion of the tramp at the coast you have two options. Turn around and return to the road end, or get a plane or helicopter. The drawback of the former option is that your four-day tramp turns into an eight-day tramp, with commensurate additions to the weight of your pack. The drawback of the latter is that it's expensive, although you do get a scenic flight into the bargain. And what a flight. The likely route is along the coast and then down the guts of Milford Sound. Breathtaking stuff indeed. Prior bookings are essential for both options.

The most pleasing way to walk the track is, in my opinion, from the mountains to the sea, following the course of the river. The flight operators, however, recommend you fly in rather than fly out, as the weather can be unpredictable and planes cannot sometimes make it to pick you up. Check the long-range forecast and if it looks dodgy, fly in.

There is, however, another cheat's way to do the return walk. The Hollyford Track guided walk company use a jetboat to take their guests from the Hollyford/Pyke confluence to the end of Lake McKerrow. You can book spaces on the return trip departing from Martins Bay Lodge (around 1½ hours from the DoC hut) at around 8.30 am. If you take this option, you could conceivably walk out in a day, although it would be a big day. Failing this, you could stay the night at Hidden Falls Hut. Give the company a call to book a place on the jetboat before you go, or pop in to the Pyke Lodge, near Lake Alabaster, or Martins Bay Lodge, a 15-minute detour from the main track at the large grass clearing after the Podocarp Walk. Staff there should be able to help you out.

Tracknet
0-3-249 7777
Freephone 0800 483 262
www.tracknet.net

Air Fiordland
0-3-249 7505
www.airfiordland.co.nz

Milford Helicopters
0-3-249 7845
www.milfordsoundhelicopters.com

Hollyford Track
Freephone 0800 832 226
www.hollyfordtrack.com

DAY ONE

Cross the swingbridge over Humboldt Creek and strike out on the wide track, which was once part of the Lower Hollyford Road extension. Beware of ongaonga, the native nettle that grows beside the track here – its sting is very painful and can even be lethal. All signs of the stinger have disappeared by Eel Creek, where you get your first glimpse from outside the forest. The vegetation succession from *Trentepohlia*, the red algae growing on the disturbed boulders, through lichens, mosses, ferns,

Hollyford road end to Swamp Creek
1 hour ■ 2 km

shrubs and trees is evident all around. Down in the valley the ghostly trunks of kahikatea trees stand as decaying monuments to the changing river course and associated drainage patterns.

The next exit from the forest is at Swamp Creek, where another piece of hillside has been demolished by the elements. Views are to Mt Te Wera (2309 m), flanked by the buttressing pillars on the ridge.

Swamp Creek to Hidden Falls Hut
2 hours ■ 7 km

After Swamp Creek the forest is a mix of beech and podocarps, with a dense understorey and proliferation of ferns. Where streams intersect the track, the white foam on their bouldery drop-offs is a perfect contrast with the green surroundings.

On a long straight stretch close to the river look out for paths to the water's edge. There are some inviting shingle beaches here with expansive views of the Darran Mountains and good places to dip your feet. The breeze often wards off the sandflies.

As the sounds of Hidden Falls become audible there is a notable increase in the *Weymouthia* moss dangling from the foliage like tatters of material. It is here taking advantage of the spray from the waterfall, which you will soon see after passing the guided walk's Sunshine Hut. Continue straight ahead before crossing the swingbridge. Take extreme care on the rocks below the falls, as they are lethally slippery.

Hidden Falls, presumably named because it is hidden from the main track, drains a massive watershed. The huge boulder perched half way up the falls dissipates some of the waterfall's energy. On the far side of the creek Hidden Falls Hut stands in a wide clearing (a short signposted detour from the main track) with views down the Hollyford Valley and to the snowy Darrans opposite. It's a new hut and a good spot to linger – but not your final destination for today.

Hidden Falls Hut to Little Homer Falls
1½ hours ■ 4 km

Back on the main track, a beech bowled in a 2003 storm shows the shallow roots that grip the steep slopes. In the next section lancewood trees are present in all their growth forms. Seedlings start out with lance-like leaves protecting the entire length of the trunk, making them unpalatable, it is claimed, to browsing birds such as the now-extinct moa. When the specimen has outgrown even the tallest moa, its crown spreads and the leaves shorten so they do a better job of photosynthesising. In mature form the crown becomes multi-headed and the leaves enlarge to catch the light and out-compete other forest plants.

If you take the climb up to Little Homer Saddle (167 m) slowly, you will have time to examine the banks of *Dawsonia superba*, thought to be the world's largest terrestrial moss, growing to 50 cm tall. The first section is the steepest, and there is a lookout up to Mt Madeline (2536 m) and Mt Tutoko (2723 m), the highest mountain in Fiordland. The gradient flattens as you near the saddle. A few clearings on the descending switchbacks allow views up the valley to the toe of the Skippers Range.

Little Homer Falls, at the conclusion of the descent, is a fine waterfall forming a curtain against the dark wall. Mosses and ferns love this moisture-filled environment and frame the spectacle.

Just before the falls is a large log scattered with splinters. This was one log too many for DoC workers, who evidently used the Davey Gunn method to remove this tree from the track. No saws or chainsaws. Just gelignite.

> W. H. Homer was an original resident of Jamestown. Venturing into the hills with a swag and his dog, Monkey, he discovered Homer Saddle in 1889 and prophesied this would be the way to put a road into Milford. He even offered to excavate a tunnel for the princely sum of £2000. Government officials should have taken him up on the offer, as by 1954 when a tunnel was eventually pierced, it cost more than £500,000.

Little Homer Falls to Alabaster Hut
1¾ hours ■ 6.5 km

The track now follows the Hollyford River before heading right at the confluence of the Pyke and Hollyford Rivers, at the foot of the Skippers Range. Pass the clearing of Pyke Lodge, where the guided walk has a lodge. Occasional fence posts and wires still demarcate the perimeter of one of the clearings made by early runholder Davey Gunn.

It was in one of these cleared pastures that Davey had a most unfortunate experience. A rampant bull chased Davey towards the fence and, in his haste, Davey didn't see a splinter protruding from a blasted tree trunk and snagged his scrotum. The rip extended down his thigh and the only means he could find to sew himself up were with a darning needle and fishing twine. 'Made me a bit crook,' he later lamented.

Behind the hut is a tablet erected in memory of Gunn. This was his favourite view of his favourite mountain – Mt Madeline. Once you witness the good-looking peak framed with beech foliage you will understand why.

This next forest section is dominated by towering red beech, overtopping tree ferns and horopito. Pass the turnoff to McKerrow Island Hut and the Demon Trail – you will return to this junction tomorrow – and follow the luminescent green Pyke River upstream to Lake Alabaster.

Alabaster Hut is at the far end of the gravel shore. Nip down to the beach and check the view. Whatever the weather it is a mystical spectacle, but in overcast humid conditions the lake and its swirling mists are at their most compelling. This is the domain of the patupaiarehe (Maori bush fairies).

Lake Alabaster, or Wawahi-waka, as it was known to Maori, was one of the best sources of totara for waka hulls and vessels would be floated down the Pyke and Hollyford Rivers to Lake McKerrow, and on to the coast. The lake is 71 m deep and 7 km long.

DAVEY GUNN Davey Gunn is a Hollyford legend. If ever there was a man totally suited to his environment and lifestyle, it was Davey. His great cattle musters were famous around the world and in the 1940s Gordon Donaldson-Law journeyed all the way from England to participate, recording his experiences in the book *Hollyford Muster.*

Starting in the Kaipo Valley to the south of the Hollyford, Gunn, his dogs and musterers would trace a route to Martins Bay via the coast, cross the Hollyford River and continue along the narrow coastal strip to Big Bay. The mob would be driven through the Pyke Valley to the confluence with the Hollyford and thence to Deadmans Camp, his base near the present Gunns Camp. On the route Gunn had a series of slab huts and holding yards where cattle could put on condition before the next drive. If prices were not favourable at Mossburn, Gunn would continue to the Invercargill sales yards, making a journey totalling around 550 km. These endeavours earned an annual income of around £100.

Once returns became totally unprofitable, Gunn used the huts as lodgings for tramping parties, some on foot and others on horseback. It was during one of these trips that Gunn reached the attention of the wider world. En route to Fox Glacier in 1936, a plane carrying one of his guests nosedived into the surf at Big Bay. With assistance, Gunn was able to rescue the passengers, although one died from his injuries. Realising that medical assistance was urgently needed, Gunn set out to reach the nearest telephone at Marian Camp (at the turnoff from the Milford Road onto the Lower Hollyford Road).

After a hard day on the track, Gunn rode around the coast to Martins Bay. Then, despite having cracked ribs in the rescue, he rowed the length of Lake McKerrow in a dinghy. Now in the dark and without food, he walked up the Hollyford to raise the alarm. In 21 hours he covered a total distance of 90 km. On today's groomed track it would take a fit tramper four days to complete the equivalent journey.

Gunn's guided tramping trips continued alongside his farming ventures until on Christmas Day 1955 he was drowned in the Hollyford River. A young boy riding on the same horse was also swept away and drowned.

HOLLYFORD TRACK

Key:

- DoC hut
- Private hut
- Shelter
- ——— Main track
- – – – Side track

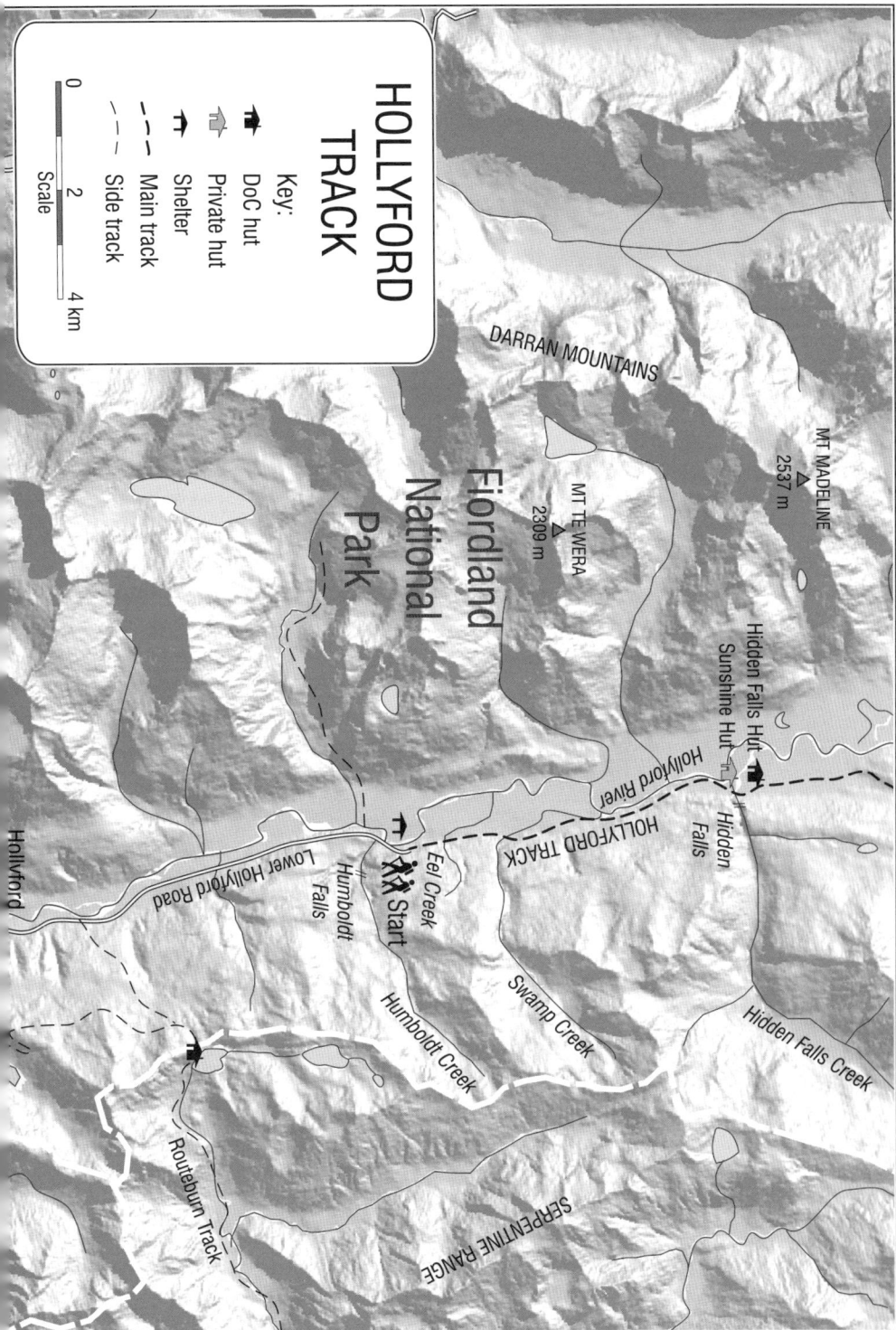

Scale
0   2   4 km

DARRAN MOUNTAINS

Fiordland
National
Park

MT MADELINE
2537 m

MT TE WERA
2309 m

Hidden Falls Hut
Sunshine Hut

Hollyford River

HOLLYFORD TRACK

Hidden
Falls

Hidden Falls Creek

Eel Creek

Start

Swamp Creek

Lower Hollyford Road

Humboldt
Falls

Humboldt Creek

SERPENTINE RANGE

Hollyford

Routeburn Track

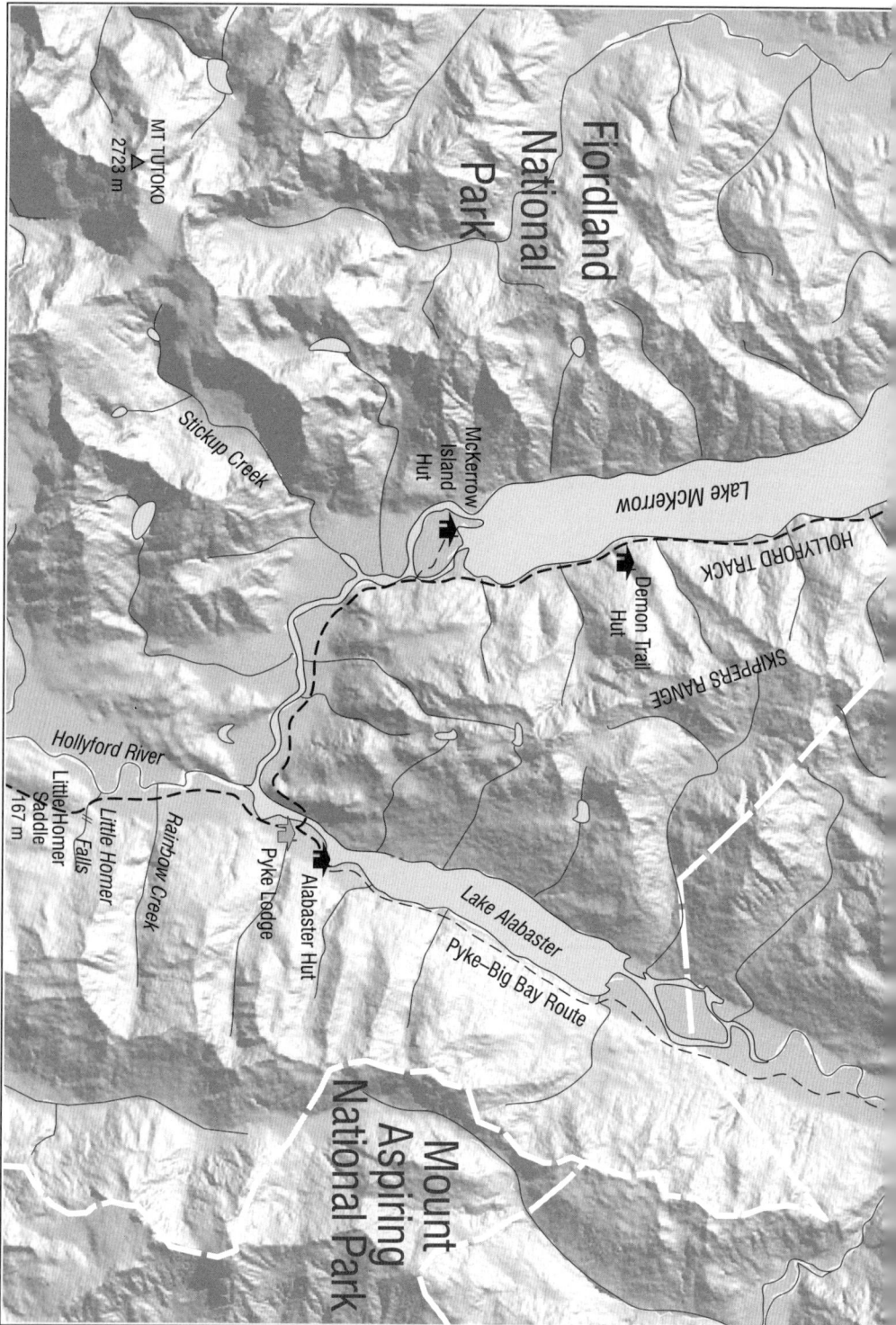

Fiordland National Park

MAY HILLS

Long Reef
Martins Bay Hut

Martins Bay

Martins Bay Lodge

Airstrip

McKenzie
Lagoon

HOLLYFORD TRACK

Podocarp Walk

Jerusalem Creek

SARA HILLS

Finish

Big Bay

Gravel
Cove

Hokuri Hut

MT WEBB
1150m

Jamestown

Hokuri Creek

Pyke River

Lake
Wilmot

N
W   E
S

DAY TWO

Alabaster Hut to McKerrow Island

3 hours ■ 9 km

Backtrack to the junction with the Demon Trail and cross the Pyke River swingbridge. In 1881 four early surveyors including Ronald Raymond and Freddie Fitt were working in the Hollyford Valley and arrived at the Pyke River on a tempestuous day. Needing to ferry their supplies to the far side, they canoed to the large braid just above the Pyke/Hollyford confluence, using it as a staging post. Fitt stayed on the island while Raymond paddled back for the next load. In the swirling currents, Raymond was washed downstream and drowned. It was another eight days before Fitt could get off the island. He survived by batting down fantails and tomtits with a stick, eating each meagre mouthful raw. Hunger, however, was not the worst of his problems. Having disrobed for the swim to safety, the sandflies were such a menace he was said to have been of a rather nervous disposition for the rest of his life.

After Raymond's death, the river was crossed by means of a wire attached to trees either side of river, from which dangled a cage, later replaced by a 'chair'. Both aerial vehicles worked by two pulley cables revolving over a drum, allowing trampers to pull the basket to whichever side they needed. The cable over the Pyke was sometimes so slack that Davey Gunn said it was like scaling a house once you passed the halfway point. The Fiordland National Park Board constructed a bridge in the 1960s, and the upgraded version was replaced by this cable suspension bridge in 1998 by DoC.

This bridge over the Pyke announces the beginning of the Demon Trail. This section of the track, while challenging, is not as diabolical as the title suggests. The track initially follows the Pyke River, passing the braid on which poor Freddie Fitt spent eight days. These first few minutes are a rude welcome to the Demon Trail, with slippery uneven rocks followed by waterlogged sections that after rain will wet the thighs. There are numerous boot-high mud sections as well as knee-deep ponds. A mossy gully and the red beech forest are the main distractions, but it pays to concentrate on your feet.

The track follows a flat shelf beside the Hollyford River at the toe of the Skippers Range. There's a good view of the flood channel around McKerrow Island, just before the track junction. If it's safe to cross the channel, have a look at the kowhai forest and views up the lake. If water is flowing in the flood channel, don't cross.

McKerrow Island Hut should be used as an overnight stop only if you are absolutely sure no rain will fall during the night. Trampers have been stranded there for more than a week when rising waters cut off their route to the mainland. Not much fun with only a *Woman's Weekly*, Gideon Bible and a Reader's Digest condensed volume for mental sustenance.

After McKerrow Island there are two walkwires and a few tricky creek crossings. The track skirts the Lake McKerrow beach briefly before undulating its way to Demon Trail Hut. The hut gets the best views of all, perched in its clearing opposite the smaller peaks of the Darrans. This is a track section where you really get your head down and concentrate on walking. There is little to see in the forest and few views out.

McKerrow Island to Demon Trail Hut
2 hours ■ 5.5 km

DAY THREE

On this section there are many undulations where the track heads away from Lake McKerrow and steeply uphill. The rocks are very slippery and you may have to carefully place your boots in the water-filled hollows between individual rocks. There are frequent windfalls, some forming elegant arches over the track, others just being a pain. You may need to crawl, take your pack off, scrape your inner thighs or just jump to get around them. At times the distinction between track and creek bed is blurred. In fact occasionally there is no distinction.

Demon Trail Hut to Hokuri Hut
6 hours ■ 9.5 km

The real highlights of this section are the walkwires, which cross racing creeks of foaming water. Some span 20 m or more and hover a good 10 m above the creek. Approximate timings between walkwires are 1 hour, 1½ hours, 1¼ hours, 30 minutes and 1 hour.

The walkwires are often in clearings, where Lake McKerrow and the Darran Mountains are well displayed. The Darrans rise very steeply from the far edge of the lake and are laced with waterfalls during rain. Hokuri Hut was recently upgraded in a new clearing and enjoys views through kiekie-decorated trees to the lake.

DAY FOUR

Hokuri Hut to Podocarp Walk

2 hours ▪ 5.5 km

After Hokuri Hut there's 30 minutes of boggy track, with slippery rocks and occasional creeks. Hokuri Creek can be crossed easily at the mouth during low flow. In high water, head 15 minutes upstream to a walkwire.

The Alpine Fault is clearly visible on the opposite shore of Lake McKerrow to Hokuri Creek. The fault runs down the gut, marred with the scars of various slips, runs under Lake McKerrow and out past Hokuri Creek to the Jamestown Saddle. After the creek crossing, the track follows the beach on the northern shore of Lake McKerrow. The kowhai flower in spring, but browsing by possums and deer has defoliated the upper and lower branches. Around 20 minutes further is a perfect semi-circular cove, with a sign reading 'Jamestown' hidden in the forest to the right. About 30 m from the sign, look for a well-trodden track leading into the

JAMESTOWN

James Macandrew had a plan. What better way, the exuberant and somewhat shady superintendent of Otago wondered, could there be to carve his name in history than to open up a much-needed port on the west coast of the province – and name the town after himself? At the time, the Australians owned the banks, and gold from the Otago goldfields had to be transported to Melbourne via the treacherous waters of Foveaux Strait. A port at Martins Bay and a road link to Queenstown would simplify the journey.

Despite initial misgivings about the practicality of constructing a road over such rough terrain, the plans for the settlement gained momentum. In early 1870 the paddle-steamer *Charles Edward* arrived at Martins Bay, at the mouth of the Hollyford River, with a government survey party to lay out the town. After several attempts to negotiate the notoriously difficult bar, they safely entered the Lower Hollyford, only for the vessel to snag on a submerged log and partially sink. The omens were not good.

Aboard the *Charles Edward* was Robert Whitworth of the *Otago Daily Times*. He waxed lyrical on the splendours of the 'beautiful half-moon bay' and the potential for an idyllic settlement. 'Martins Bay will ere long, become one of the most promising [settlements] in Otago; what is now a wild impassable bush, will be dotted with smiling homesteads and the dark and tangled forest-covered flats will be transformed into verdant meadows and fields of golden grain,' he wrote.

The site chosen for Jamestown was a few kilometres inland, on the shore of Lake McKerrow, and the first settlers arrived on the *Esther Ann* in July 1870. A severe gale whipped in over the Tasman and blew the vessel onto the point of the sandspit, from where she slewed onto rocks forest. Here is a plaque showing the site of Jamestown and the decaying apple trees that are the last remaining evidence of the failed settlement. The rusting paraphernalia is from later endeavours.

Back at the lake, the beach has carved into shelves at differing lake levels. You will have to negotiate rocky promontories and tussle with manuka and flax, but generally it is easy going. It's a treat to be out of the forest among the lake views for the first time in two days.

Bottlenose dolphins sometimes swim up from the sea to the lake. It's thought they hunt trout here, possibly using knowledge passed down through the generations from the days when the old hunting ground was still a fiord. Sea fish would have been abundant and parents would have taught youngsters the value of feeding here. The unique Milford and Doubtful bottlenose dolphins grow to 4.5 m long and have short beaks. They are black and white with a hooked dorsal fin.

Eventually you will come to a corrugated-iron shack at the start of the Podocarp Walk.

and was wrecked. There was no loss of life but the settlers lost all their personal effects and the materials for a sawmill.

When word got out that four out of the first five vessels to attempt to cross the Hollyford Bar had come unstuck, ships' captains started refusing to take their vessels over the bar – insurance would not cover it. Progress on constructing the town's other lifeline, a road to Queenstown, was painfully slow.

The settlers had to endure extreme isolation and frequent floods, and the land was not good for farming. By 1872 the hardy residents were beginning to starve and some mothers were boiling sea kelp to feed their children. William Henry Homer was sent over to Queenstown to enlighten the powers that be of their plight. After an arduous journey that resulted in his near collapse from exhaustion, Homer arrived an emaciated wreck. On demanding from Macandrew a remedy to their hardships, he received a chilly riposte. There was to be no scheduled steamer service and no road. Jamestown was sunk.

The settlers slowly drifted away and by 1879 the town was all but deserted. A few settlers stayed on, among them the Webb family. William Webb had arrived with the pioneer group in 1870 and married Amelia Gaudin in the only marriage to take place in the settlement. They had four children, two of whom died after eating some 'bright coloured berries'. Amelia then lost a premature baby soon after birth. In 1896, as the family readied themselves to leave Jamestown, their eldest son succumbed to influenza. It is said William Webb didn't look back as the *Hinemoa* departed Martins Bay and the failed settlement.

Podocarp Walk to Jerusalem Creek
1½ hours ■ 4 km

The shack at the beginning of this section houses a waka (canoe). This unlikely find has an interesting story behind it. In 1999 massive flooding struck Fiordland, dislodging the waka from its resting place at the bottom of Lake McKerrow. It was discovered by a party from the guided walk and hauled to the bank. The Department of Conservation invited Ngai Tahu representatives to inspect the waka. With a cursory glance the elders could tell it wasn't one of theirs – the workmanship was rough, it had a square seat at the stern and it was made from kahikatea using square-head nails. It was most likely hewn by early European explorers, probably as a vehicle for crossing the Hollyford River.

The Podocarp Walk takes you through forest where rata vines entwine their hosts in such dense curtains that at times you cannot see the trunks. The rimu encountered after 10 minutes is so choked by vines it's a wonder it survives. A puka perches in the branch clefts and numerous epiphytes blanket the branches. This tree could be around a thousand years old. About 10 minutes further, to the right of the track, there are two more fine rimu with open structures and massive crowns. Look also for white rata on the coprosmas in the disturbed forest further on.

Cross the large grassy clearing past the guided walkers' Martins Bay Lodge and the airstrip. The Sara (north) and May (south) Hills guard the mouth of the river. You now enter a bizarre forest, mainly composed of tutu and wineberry. This forest is around 40 years old and has grown up on disturbed land flooded by nearby Jerusalem Creek. Large asparagus-like shoots rise from the tutu like spears and the intensity of green in the forest interior is almost fluorescent. Ignore the sign to the Air Fiordland airstrip and continue to Jerusalem Creek.

Jerusalem Creek to Martins Bay Hut
1½ hours ■ 4 km

Jerusalem Creek can be higher than knee-deep in heavy rain. The river bed has been filled with gravel washed down from the Sara Hills and the land level is constantly rising with the addition of new material. This accumulation of debris has been responsible for closing off the mouth of the Hollyford River, creating a large expanse of flat land and damming Lake McKerrow. This has happened in the last 6500 years – before that Lake McKerrow was the northernmost fiord.

Around 30 m after the climb look out for the sycamore tree on the left, slightly back from the track. Here lies John Robertson, the postman for Jamestown. During the 1870s, Jerusalem Creek was in fact named Robertsons Creek. For the generous sum of £100 per year, Robertson made a monthly mail run to Queenstown, a journey of over a week each way. After years enduring constantly soaked clothing, eating little in the way of fresh produce and being forced to extreme physical exertions, Robertson succumbed to tuberculosis and died in 1882.

On the consolidated dunes behind the estuarine river mouth the forest character changes again. Crown ferns grow in profusion on the forest floor and multi-trunked kamahi rise to a dense canopy that hogs all the light. The sound of the ocean beckons, a promise soon realised with lookouts over the river, Tasman Sea and Martins Bay spit.

The track drops down to Flax Creek, which can rise rapidly in heavy rain and is a popular meeting place for hungry sandflies in calm conditions. On the climb out, look behind you at the classic west coast view – nikau palms, dense forest, the receding valley and snow-capped Tutoko piercing the skyline. Continue along the dunes until you near the river mouth.

Just inside the sand bar a sign indicates the lower boat landing, where vessels moored in times past. Coastal vegetation now dominates the trackside. A fine view takes in the length of the spit and the occasional fur seal basking on the rocks.

The beach just before the hut gives the best views up the Hollyford Valley, with the bar and spit at the conclusion. The waters are rarely calm and many of the rocks once peppering the entrance have since been blasted. It's obvious this river mouth was never going to be navigable, and Jamestown was always doomed.

At Martins Bay Hut your journey to the sea is complete – but there is still Long Reef to be explored.

> The dune systems of the Martins Bay spit are completely unmodified, save a few rabbit, deer and stoat prints on the sand. The transition of ecosystems from estuary to forest through dunelands, wetland and lagoon is inconspicuous. McKenzies Lagoon, only visible from the air, is home to New Zealand scaup, Australasian bittern and black swans. Pingao is the dominant dune binder and other plants include muttonbird scrub, which reaches its northern limit here.

From the hut navigate through the flax corridor to a sign announcing the start of the Pyke–Big Bay route. This is in the clearing occupied by the old DoC hut, behind a large boulder. *Dracophyllum longifolium* and kiekie are conspicuous. As you clamber through mud and over rocks and steps, spare a thought for the McKenzies, who cut this track in the 1870s.

Long Reef
2 hours ■ 4 km return

The small bay between the headland and Long Reef funnels the waves and in a monster swell is an impressive sight. It is possible to walk along the beach to bypass some of the uglier track sections, but be aware of the state of the tide. The safer track negotiates the foot of the hill, then descends to Long Reef through a forest of toetoe. It's a muddy obstacle course to get to the reef, which marks the northern boundary of Fiordland National Park. The main residents you are likely to encounter here are fur seals and, at some times of year, Fiordland crested penguins.

New Zealand fur seals were hunted nearly to extinction in the early 19th century but are making a comeback. From late October bulls stake out their territory. They grow up to 1.8 m long and tip the scales at 160 kg, so imagine the fracas when two have a go at each other. It makes a heavyweight title fight look like a playground scuffle. They do not even enter the water to feed until mid January.

Females give birth in December and January, then receive the males within six days of giving birth. Tough deal! Pups are dependent for nearly a year. Another tough deal! Most feed on octopus, squid, hoki, barracouta and lanternfish. They can dive up to 200 m. At mid to low tides pups often play in the rock pools and are indifferent to human presence.

Although generally tolerant, fur seals are known to chase and bite, especially when pups are young. Keep 20 m away and if they show any distress, retreat. Try not to get between a seal and the sea, as this is its escape route. The best *modus operandi* is to find a rock to perch on and do as the seals do. Lie quietly as if in slumber.

Fiordland crested penguins grow to 40 cm tall and weigh 3 kg. Their total population is estimated at around 2500. They can use their strong beaks to climb steep bush slopes and have been seen at 100 m above sea level. They have a raucous braying call that you may hear echoing off the large boulders and intermingling with the surf.

In July they come ashore to breed in colonies of two to 50 pairs. They nest in caves or under large boulders and are most often encountered by surprise while exploring Long Reef. Their simple hollows are made from sticks and leaves. In August one or two eggs are laid and both parents share the incubation for 31 to 36 days. After hatching, the males stand guard while females head out to fish. The females regurgitate semi-digested offerings of fish and squid to their progeny, which are fully fledged by November when they go to sea.

In February the adult penguins revisit their nesting site for a 25-day moult, during which they cannot move, swim or eat and have trouble keeping warm. They are literally sitting penguins for predators. If you come across a bird in moult, stay well clear, as the poor thing is having a hard enough time as it is, without a camera-touting tramper intruding. From March to June they stay at sea before repeating the cycle.

ROUTEBURN TRACK

39 km ■ three days ■ one way ■ Great Walk

For all-encompassing views from the tops, the Routeburn on a good day is hard to beat. The breathtaking panoramas from Key Summit and Conical Hill are well known in tramping circles, with around 11,000 trampers annually walking the track.

It's a steady climb on day one, initially to Key Summit for 360-degree views of the Darran Mountains, the Hollyford Valley and the way ahead. The track drops to Lake Howden, perfect for lingering on a sunny day, then passes Earland Falls and the Orchard on the way to Lake Mackenzie and the hut. Emily and Ocean Peaks tower behind the emerald waters.

On day two there's a steep ascent to the spur, with extensive views along the Darrans and to the coast at Martins Bay. The track hugs the Hollyford Bluffs high above the treeline before reaching the essential detour up Conical Hill, above Harris Saddle. On the eastern side of the saddle the track drops past Lake Harris to the Routeburn Falls Hut.

Day three continues the descent to Routeburn Flats, where there are fine views up towards Mt Somnus. Passing through silver beech forest with some interesting rock formations, the track then follows the Route Burn (river) to the shelter at the road end.

The Routeburn Track has a long and intriguing history. The route was once followed by Maori travellers making their way between villages on the coast such as Kotuku at Martins Bay and inland settlements. Those early travellers traded pounamu, as well as kiwi and kakapo feathers, for muttonbirds, mere (flat clubs), adzes and fish hooks. They gave names stretching from the lake Wakatipu through Te Komama (Route Burn) to Tarahaka Whakatipu (Harris Saddle) and Whakatipu Waitai (Lake McKerrow). The name of the region was Titiraurangi, meaning 'land of many peaks piercing the clouds'.

In 1863 government prospector Patrick Quirk Caples, in search of payable gold, travelled up the Route Burn from the Dart Valley along a route roughly following today's track. He named Lake Harris and Harris Saddle, before continuing to the Hollyford Valley. A road following this route to the west coast at Martins Bay was begun, but in the face of technical challenges and mounting costs, work ceased after four years.

In the last two decades of the 19th century, as tourism started to creep into the lives of the station owners at the head of Lake Wakatipu, guided parties began exploring the Route Burn. A teenager called

SECTION TIMINGS

DAY ONE 6 hours 15 km

The Divide to Key Summit turnoff	1 hour	3 km
Key Summit (optional)	1 hour	2.5 km return
Key Summit turnoff to Howden Hut	15 min	1 km
Howden Hut to Earland Falls	1¼ hours	3 km
Earland Falls to Mackenzie Hut	2¼ hours	5.5 km

DAY TWO 6½ hours 14.5 km

Lake Mackenzie Hut to Harris Saddle	3½ hours	8 km
Conical Hill (optional)	1¼ hours	3 km return
Harris Saddle to Routeburn Falls Hut	1½ hours	3.5 km

DAY THREE 3 hours 9 km

Routeburn Falls Hut to Routeburn Flats Hut	1 hour	2.5 km
Routeburn Flats Hut to Routeburn Shelter	2 hours	6.5 km

Harry Bryant, along with Harry Birley from Glenorchy, would accompany tourists on an overnight horse trek up to Harris Saddle. After traversing the gorge on a benched track above the Route Burn, riders would enter the Routeburn Flats and the hut, where they camped for the night. The following morning the journey continued on foot with a grunty climb to the bushline and Lake Harris, the source of the Route Burn. Skirting the lake, these first trampers would scramble up the rocky bluff behind the lake to the saddle and take in the view.

In 1912 the minister of tourism, Thomas Mackenzie, enthused about the possibility of extending the track from Harris Saddle to Lake Howden. Harry Birley explored a route and discovered Lake Mackenzie in the process. Tom Bryant, brother of Harry, was entrusted with the task of supplying the track-building gangs. Prince, one of his packhorses, nearly came a cropper one day near the saddle when he became jammed in a rock crevice with precipitous drops on either side. Bryant was able to unload the gear and repack the horse to continue the journey, but not without a drop of perspiration or two. The peat bogs near Lake Harris turned to quagmires with the repeated hoof falls, making Bryant feel he was earning his pay.

Early trampers steamed up Wakatipu aboard the same *Earnslaw* that chugs up the lake today. With the construction of the Queenstown Glenorchy Road in 1962, the Routeburn was opened up to buses. Trampers were entertained by a commentary as the vehicles hugged the mountainsides. Buses were often filled to double capacity, which on one occasion contributed to a broken stringer on a bridge's deck. Although the service was haphazard, the general joviality radiated through the trampers and readied them for their journey along the Routeburn Track.

This description applies to walking the track from the Divide. Most people, however, attempt the track in the other direction, starting from the Queenstown end.

BOOKING

As this is a DoC Great Walk, all accommodation, both huts and camping, must be booked in advance (www.doc.govt.nz). There are four huts on the tramp (Howden Hut 28 bunks, Lake Mackenzie Hut 50 bunks,

Routeburn Falls Hut 48 bunks, Routeburn Flats Hut 20 bunks) with campsites at Routeburn Flats and Lake Mackenzie.

It is also possible to walk the track with guides, staying in private lodges along the way. Contact www.ultimatehikes.co.nz.

Terralink's Greenstone & Routeburn Tracks map is the best for this area. DoC's Routeburn & Greenstone Trackmap 335-02 is also available.

GETTING THERE

The walk starts at the Divide, 83.5 km from Te Anau along the Milford Road. Tracknet runs four daily services from Te Anau at around 7 am, 9.30 am, 11 am and 1.15 pm. Return services depart the Divide at 10.15 am, 1.30 pm, 3.15 pm and 5.45 pm. Tracknet also runs connections between Te Anau and Queenstown, departing Te Anau at 5 pm or Queenstown at 4.30 pm. Reservations are essential.

The other end of the track is at the Routeburn Shelter. From Queenstown, follow the road to Glenorchy then the Glenorchy Routeburn Road until you cross the Dart River. Turn right onto Routeburn Road and continue to the shelter at the road end.

From November to April, Info & Track runs daily shuttles departing 37 Shotover St, Queenstown, at 8 am and 12.30 pm, arriving in Glenorchy an hour later and the Routeburn an hour after that. Return services depart the Routeburn Shelter at 10 am, 2 pm and 4.45 pm. Reservations are essential.

Tracknet
0-3-249 7777
Freephone 0800 483 262
www.tracknet.net

Info & Track
0-3-442 9708
www.infotrack.co.nz

DAY ONE

The Divide to Key Summit turnoff
1 hour ■ 3 km

The first section of the walk to Key Summit is the most popular of the longer day walks off the Milford Road, but if you avoid the 11 am to 2 pm pulse, the rush is barely noticeable. The well-used and even track is a steady climb from 530 m at the Divide to 919 m at Key Summit.

Numerous small rivulets cascade down the hillside, on which stands dense, well-watered silver beech forest smothered with *Weymouthia* moss. As you approach the bushline, mountain flax, alpine totara and dracophyllum are among the alpine species.

Be sure to take the detour to Key Summit, as few places summon such vast, enthralling views. To the north is the Hollyford Valley, flanked to the east by the Ailsa Mountains and to the west by the Darrans. Above the Lake Marian bowl is the pyramid-shaped Mt Christina and serrated Mt Crosscut. Looking east from the Lake Marian lookout is the Greenstone Valley, with the Eglinton sneaking in to the south.

Key Summit
1 hour ▪
2.5 km return

    The European name of Key Summit refers to the fact it is the 'key' to three watersheds. A drop of rain falling on Key Summit may end up in one of three oceans. Should it head south it will flow into Lake Fergus, Lake Gunn and the Eglinton River, then pass through Lake Te Anau to the Upper Waiau and into Lake Manapouri. If we conveniently forget about the possibility of its being diverted through the power station into Doubtful Sound, then our drop of rain will continue through the Waiau River to Te Waewae Bay and the Southern Ocean. If the raindrop heads north, it will reach the Hollyford River and flow into Lake McKerrow and then continue to the Tasman Sea. If by some quirk it heads east into the Greenstone River, it will travel through Lake Wakatipu, down the Kawarau to Cromwell and into the Clutha River, eventually reaching the Pacific Ocean at Balclutha.

From the junction the track descends to Howden Hut through a forest composed almost entirely of silver beech. It is hard to see the bark of the trunks and branches, such is the coating of moss. In the early morning, before the sun has risen over the peaks, or in the wet, old man's beard lichen glows like fairy lights, illuminating the form of the branches.

Key Summit turnoff to Howden Hut
15 min ▪ 1 km

    A break at the hut gives time to digest the views of the surrounding peaks of the Ailsa Mountains while listenting to the sound of the rippling stream emanating from Lake Howden. Black swans forage in the cool waters while kakariki and tui enliven the forest rim.

Beyond Howden Hut the mossy silver beech forest could be the haunt of a hobbit or the stamping ground of a leprechaun, such is the profusion of green and abundance of drooping branches. A number of delightful cascades trickle down through the forest and emanate in sprays of white.

Howden Hut to Earland Falls
1¼ hours ▪ 3 km

ROUTEBURN TRACK

Key:
- DoC hut
- Private hut
- Shelter
- Main track
- Side track

Scale
0   2   4 km

Fiordland National Park

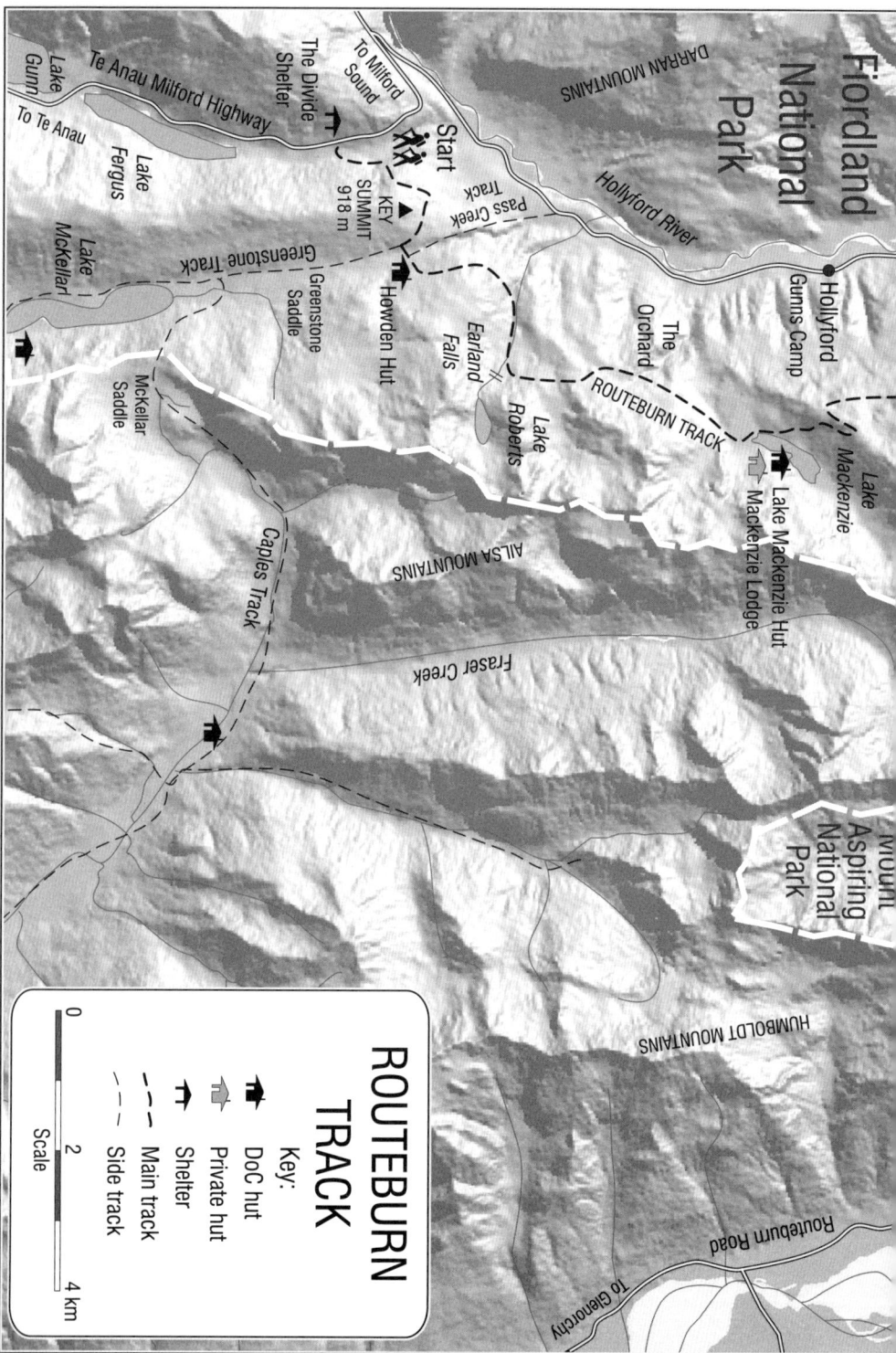

DARRAN MOUNTAINS

Hollyford River

Hollyford
Gunns Camp

To Milford Sound
The Divide Shelter
Te Anau Milford Highway
To Te Anau
Lake Gunn
Lake Fergus
Lake McKellar

Start
KEY SUMMIT 918 m
Pass Creek Track
Greenstone Track
Greenstone Saddle
Howden Hut
Earland Falls
Lake Roberts
The Orchard
ROUTEBURN TRACK
Lake Mackenzie
Lake Mackenzie Hut
Mackenzie Lodge

McKellar Saddle
Caples Track
AILSA MOUNTAINS
Fraser Creek

Mount Aspiring National Park
HUMBOLDT MOUNTAINS

Routeburn Road
To Glenorchy

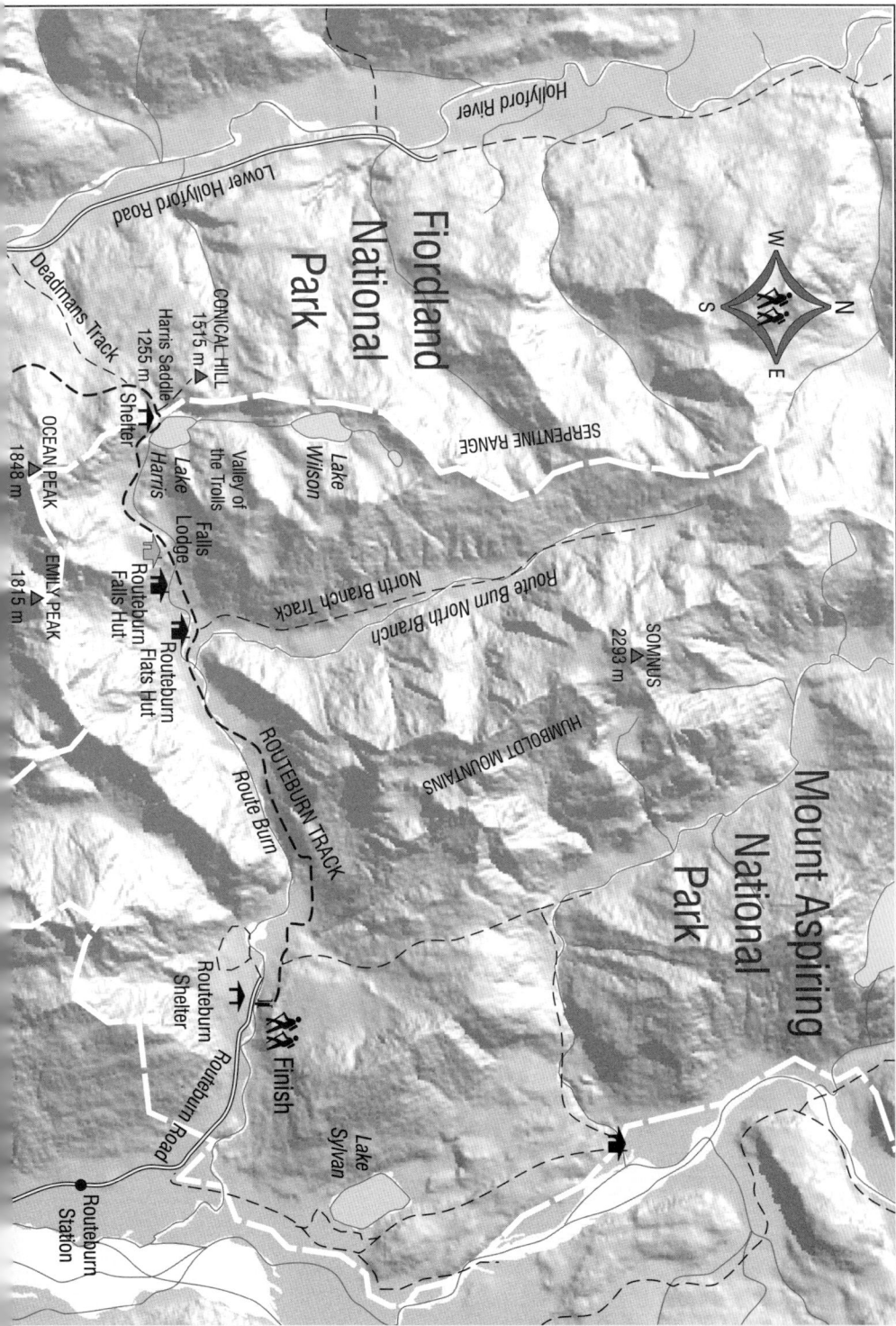

They are often bordered by a mat of intensely green mosses that show off the dripping water. Orchids inhabit the banks.

For the most part the views of the Darrans are tantalisingly concealed behind the Japanese-style architecture of the silver beech. Then, after an hour, the audible rush of the Earland Falls draws the gaze skyward to where the falls disgorge through a cleft in the rock.

The 174 m falls spread on their descent so by the time the water reaches the base it is just bursts of spray. The force of the falls creates a wind that sends the spray over the surrounding forest and rocks. Take care as the surfaces are slippery. The streams emptying the pool weave around rocks and to get a good photo, you need to crouch in the lee of the spray and poke your camera up as a sniper would shoot his prey.

Earland Falls to Lake Mackenzie Hut
2¼ hours ▪ 5.5 km

A delicate sphagnum garden with *Dracophyllum menziesii* and ourisia inhabits the rocks on the trackside beyond Earland Falls. Before long you will come to a clearing caused by a landslip and now colonised by hebes and wineberry. The clearing allows the first extensive view down the Darrans, a view you will never get used to. Major peaks from the Milford Road end include Mt Christina, Mt Crosscut, Mt Te Wera, Mt Madeline and Mt Tutoko.

Behind there are views back to Earland Falls. Put a waterfall like this in a country like England and it would be a major tourist attraction, with coach park and tearooms to boot. In Fiordland such beauty is commonplace but never to be taken for granted.

The track dips in and out of the forest. A deep rumbling bass note creeps into the forest and for a few moments could trick the tramper into thinking an earthquake was imminent. It is in fact another water feature echoing off the cleft walls and resonating with force. Other smaller rods of water dive off nearby boulders in a confusion of cascades. Take a look behind you shortly after for the view of the scene and Earland Falls.

The track stays mainly in the forest for 45 minutes on the way to the Orchard, aptly named as this clearing filled with ribbonwood trees could be mistaken for a Somerset apple orchard. The first views to Lake McKerrow open up at the head of the Hollyford Valley with the spurs of the Skippers Range receding in misty tones. This is quite a sight.

The track weaves in and out of the forest, then drops over a footbridge and a deep gouge in the rock. Astelia with bizarre scribble marks on the leaves attract the eye before the track enters a section of silver beech forest where the sizeable trees have no branches, only an open crown hogging the light at the canopy. Cushion mosses soften the trunks' contours.

The clearing before Lake Mackenzie Hut is filled with hebes. Pass the guided walk hut before you come to Lake Mackenzie Hut and the lake. Be prepared for an idyll. The rocks scattered beside the lake are joined by countless colleagues beneath the green waters, which lead up to Ocean and Emily Peaks.

From Lake Mackenzie Hut, there is a side track towards the campsite. After a 400 m section over high rocky bluffs (to be replaced with a gantry) the new campsite is near the lake. The track continues to Leaning Rock.

DAY TWO

The track leads through an assortment of boulders that have peeled off the bluffs. Densely packed silver beech trees create a shady maze. Suddenly the track pokes above the treeline and Lake Mackenzie, Ocean Peak and Emily Peak fill the view. The mountainside is clothed with celmisias, whipcord hebes, dracophyllum, speargrass and Mount Cook lilies.

Lake Mackenzie Hut to Harris Saddle
3½ hours ■ 8 km

Orange marker poles lead in zigzags up the face, which takes around 1¼ hours to climb. At the apex of the spur is another Routeburn treat, probably the widest panorama on the main track. The view stretches from the Earl Mountains all the way to the coast at Martins Bay, a distance of over 50 km. All the major peaks of the Darrans are there, with glaciers descending from the summit peaks. If you are here in the evening, the low angle of the sun striking through the cols on the Darrans will provide a dusky view. The light also reflects off Emily Peak and the southern side of the Mackenzie bowl.

The section along the Hollyford Bluffs is exposed, as you are well above the treeline. The track is benched into the mountainside with the summits of the Serpentine Range not far above and the vastness of the Hollyford Valley below. Each headland is followed by another and the views behind are as enticing as those ahead. It's a privilege to be here on a fine day. But if you catch the bluffs section on a bad day, the journey will be arduous and at times you'll be thankful for the marker poles.

After 1 hour Deadmans Track heads down into the valley to the left while the main track continues for 30 minutes to its high point at Harris Saddle. The shelter is a lifesaver on a rough day.

Conical Hill
1¼ hours ■ 3 km return

In a tramp filled with views, this is *the* viewpoint. It's around 260 m to the summit of this oddly shaped hill, a smoothed hummock of rock on the range. The climb is a rocky old track with some nice cobbled track work at the start near the shelter. Poles are anchored into the rock.

At the top you can tick off the Darrans peaks, including Mt Madeline and Mt Tutoko. Moraine Creek, leading up to Lake Adelaide, is clearly visible. The view stretches to Lake Gunn in the east and to Martins Bay, at the mouth of the Hollyford Valley, in the west.

Harris Saddle to Routeburn Falls Hut
1½ hours ■ 3.5 km

On the other side of the saddle the track sidles the bowl above Lake Harris. It's a strange terrain of hummocky smoothed rock and tussock (mainly *Chionochloa spiralis*). The far side of the lake is called the Valley of Trolls, where the bizarre rock formations could certainly be the lair of a troll, ready to eat you for dinner.

The track perches on bluffs above Lake Harris and has been laboriously cut into the rock. It's clear how misguided the early pioneers were in trying to build a road over the Harris Saddle. A road indeed! Jamestown was certainly doomed when you consider how tough conditions would have been, even on a fine day.

The lake is in a cirque scoured out of the rock by the head of a glacier and large boulders are strewn about the alpine meadows. In late summer the sweet scent of ribbonwood, with its pretty white flowers, wafts through the air, crickets leap between rocks and tussock swirls in the warm breeze.

Lake Harris spills gently into the Route Burn via a cascade. This sound of running water accompanies your descent through the meadows. Views of Mt Earnslaw's lower slopes start to open up ahead, then culminate in a viewpoint above Routeburn Falls Hut. This is probably the most photographed spot on the tramp. The perspective down the Route Burn is memorable, with a steep spur forcing the wide braided river into a sinuous course. The valley flats are hemmed with a dense silver beech forest.

The Routeburn Falls find numerous paths through the smoothed rock, winding though clefts to the valley floor. Both the public Routeburn Falls Hut and the guided walkers' lodge are close by.

DAY THREE

The track drops into the silver beech forest where the trees are, unusually, immediately lofty. Generally at the treeline the silver beech are stunted and moss covered. A short section of towering red beech occupies a better drained site. The track crosses Emily Creek on a swingbridge. Other footbridges give vantage points along other creeks.

Routeburn Falls Hut to Routeburn Flats Hut
1 hour ■ 2.5 km

From the large slip created during a 1994 storm, there are impressive views up the Route Burn North Branch to Mt Somnus (2293 m), with its permanent snowfields, glacier and broad gully – a skier's El Dorado. The slip has created a graveyard of dead trunks. Debris is still loose, so take care when crossing the slip. Where the track circumvents Phoenix Bluff, again keep an eye out, especially in heavy rain.

The track descends to a junction with the track to Routeburn Flats Hut, 5 minutes to the left. Beautifully sited on the flats with Route Burn North Branch and Mt Somnus in view, this is the New Zealand of tourist brochures. The campsite is 200 m upstream.

Skirting the grassy Routeburn Flats at the bush edge before re-entering the forest, this section is almost entirely through silver beech forest, with the track following the Route Burn. There are two swingbridges, the second catching views up the bouldery stream.

Routeburn Flats Hut to Routeburn Shelter
2 hours ■ 6.5 km

Forge Flat is a sunny beach by the ice-blue waters of the river. This is a popular spot to linger for lunch, throw rocks in the water and listen to the crashing that results.

A section known as Sappers Pass is just one of the undulations on the wide smooth track cultivated for day walkers. Before long the Route Burn suddenly seems to end in a barricade of rocks and tree trunks. The entire river dives out of view though a narrow gap in the rock before re-emerging into the wide flats.

A large wooden bridge on steel girders spans a set of canyons, with the force of water excavating small chasms in the rock. Canyoners belay each other through torrents while clipped to the rock faces. Through the forest foliage there are peeks towards the Dart Valley, with a high vertical cliff face on the right.

It is now an easy path back to the swingbridge over the river and the road. The Routeburn Shelter is 200 m up the road on the right, with an open fire for wet days or a grassy flat for sunny summer days, when the Routeburn Track is at its best.

GREENSTONE AND CAPLES TRACKS

55 km ■ four days ■ loop

The Greenstone and Caples Valleys, connected at the confluence of the rivers near Lake Wakatipu and at McKellar Saddle, can be linked with a four-day tramp. Both valleys are wide with flat unforested bottoms, making travel relatively easy, and open to views of the high peaks of the surrounding ranges. Much of the walk passes through the Greenstone Conservation Area, an area of private land that embodies all the grand scenery of Fiordland but with a hint of Mount Aspiring National Park.

Day one follows the grassy pastoral flats of the Caples Valley with high snow-covered peaks for a backdrop. This is the New Zealand of postcards, with cattle grazing lush pastures in view of majestic peaks. After a night at the Upper Caples Hut, there's the hardest section to McKellar Saddle. The track is rough as it climbs through silver beech forest to a boardwalk over alpine vegetation. There are fine views of Mt Christina and the Earl Mountains before the steep descent to the wide Greenstone Valley and a second night at McKellar Hut.

On day three the track gently descends the open grassed valley towards the toe of the Ailsa Mountains. There is time to take in the Livingstone Mountains and the sublime scenery. A short detour over a bridged gorge leads to the night's accommodation, the new Greenstone Hut. On day four you will pass through a selection of beech forest and enter the gorge of the lower Greenstone River. Towering Tooth Peak shades the confluence with the Caples River – from here you return to the shores of Lake Wakatipu.

Europeans first explored this area in March 1861 when Southland runholders George Gunn and David McKellar travelled up the Mararoa and Greenstone Valleys. In search of pastures new, they came upon in the Greenstone Valley 'a beautiful lake entirely surrounded by bush' that now goes by the name of Lake McKellar. They spied evidence of gardens on the shores, indicating that this area may have been a pit stop for the Maori greenstone traders who travelled up the valley. After crossing the inconspicuous Greenstone Saddle, Gunn and McKellar stumbled upon Lake Howden. From Key Summit they could make out a chain of three lakes (probably Lakes Lochie, Fergus and Gunn) and were awed by the audible power of the avalanches roaring down Mt Crosscut into Lake Marian. After a few days on the tops, they mistook Lake McKerrow for

SECTION TIMINGS

DAY ONE 5 hours 13 km

Greenstone road end to Greenstone/Caples track junction	30 min	2 km
Greenstone/Caples Track junction to Mid Caples Hut	2½ hours	5 km
Mid Caples Hut to Upper Caples Hut	2 hours	6 km

DAY TWO 5 hours 14.5 km

Upper Caples Hut to McKellar Saddle	3 hours	9.5 km
McKellar Saddle to Caples/Greenstone track junction	1 hour	2 km
Caples/Greenstone track junction to McKellar Hut	1 hour	3 km

DAY THREE 6 hours 17 km

McKellar Hut to Steele Creek	4 hours	11 km
Steele Creek to Greenstone Hut	2 hours	6 km

DAY FOUR 2½ hours 10 km

Greenstone Hut to Greenstone/Caples track junction	2 hours	8 km
Greenstone/Caples track junction to Greenstone road end	30 min	2 km

the coast before retreating with the conviction that the region was too heavily timbered for their purposes.

In 1863 Patrick Quirk Caples ascended the Greenstone Valley on the way to his first European east–west crossing of Otago. Government geologist James Hector was another early European traveller in the Greenstone, although his proposal for a road up the valley was rejected in favour of the hopelessly ambitious Harris Saddle route. The easy contours, fine scenery and connection with the Otago interior made the Greenstone and Caples Valleys easy choices for this important east–west thoroughfare. Today, while following in the footsteps of the early Maori and European travellers, there is a palpable sense of their passing.

BOOKINGS

The Greenstone and Caples Tracks are not Great Walks, so places cannot be booked. Hut tickets must be purchased in advance from a DoC centre. Space is not usually a problem except during December and January. There are four huts on the route (McKellar Hut 20 bunks, Greenstone Hut 20 bunks, Mid Caples Hut 12 bunks, Upper Caples Hut 20 bunks). You must bring your own stove. Camping is permitted along the bush edge 50 m from the track. You cannot camp on McKellar Saddle or on the open valley floors of the Caples or Greenstone Valleys – this is private land. There is no fee for camping unless you use the hut facilities.

There is also a guided walk option up the Greenstone Valley, staying in private lodges, as part of a longer walk that continues on the Routeburn Track. Contact www.ultimatehikes.co.nz.

Terralink's Greenstone & Routeburn Tracks map is the best for this area. DoC's Routeburn & Greenstone Trackmap 335-09 is also available.

GETTING THERE

The route described here starts at Greenstone Station, on Lake Wakatipu. From Queenstown, follow the road to Glenorchy then continue along Greenstone Station Road to the road end near the mouth of the

Greenstone River, where a car park, shelter and toilets are situated a little back from the lake.

During the Great Walks season, Info & Track runs daily shuttles departing 37 Shotover St, Queenstown, at 8 am and 12.30 pm, arriving in Glenorchy 1 hour later. This connects with the Backpacker Express service, which arrives at the road end 1 hour after that. Reservations are essential.

Info & Track
0-3-442 9708
www.infotrack.co.nz

Backpacker Express runs a bus service to the Greenstone road end departing Glenorchy at 9.30 am and 1.30 pm. For the return journey the service departs the road end at 10 am and 2 pm for Glenorchy, where it connects with Info & Track services back to Queenstown.

Backpacker Express
0-3-442 9939

The loop can also be joined from the western end. Follow the Milford Road 83.5 km from Te Anau to the Divide, which is also the start of the Routeburn Track and the walk to Key Summit. You will need to follow signs for Howden Hut, then deviate over the Greenstone Saddle to the junction of the Greenstone and Caples Tracks. This adds around 2½ hours each way to the tramp, not including a detour to Key Summit.

Tracknet
0-3-249 7777
Freephone 0800 483 262
www.tracknet.net

Tracknet runs three daily services at around 7 am, 9.30 am and 1.15 pm from Te Anau to the Divide.

Reservations are essential for all these services.

DAY ONE

Greenstone road end to Greenstone/ Caples track junction
30 min ▪ 2 km

The car park at the end of Greenstone Station Road has toilets and a picnic shelter with interpretation panels on the natural and human histories of the tracks. The photos of Maori backpacks and sandals are particularly interesting and a reminder that today's fancy gear and manicured tracks give us an experience far removed from that of early travellers. The landscape is the same, but the physical hardships endured are a world apart.

The walk begins with a fair rise over the spur above the final reaches of the Greenstone River, the sound of the water echoing off the valley walls below. The forest is mainly mountain beech with a smattering of red beech thrown in, the partly decayed leaves on the track surface weathered to a bright red. The track drops to a junction next to a sizeable suspension bridge.

Follow the track up the Caples Valley – you will not cross the suspension bridge until the end of your walk. The views of the snow-capped Darran Mountains will draw you up the valley with an invisible thread. With the Ailsa Mountains to the left and the Humboldts to the right, and a flat grassy valley floor, this is the New Zealand of postcards.

Greenstone/ Caples track junction to Mid Caples Hut
2½ hours ■ 5 km

This section follows the bush edge on the true left of the Caples River. Sometimes the track runs through mountain beech forest, the dappled light casting illumination onto the open understorey. When the track veers onto the flats the views open up. Remember also to look back down the valley at Tooth Peak.

The Caples River has a snaking course over the wide valley floor, striving always for that perfect sine wave. In places where deep pools occur, the water is an opal blue, dusted with a sprinkling of sunlight. Hereford cattle munch the lush pastures, a reminder we are crossing private land. The Lombardy poplars on the far side of the valley mark the site of a previous homestead.

Nearing Mid Caples Hut, the track climbs a terrace where all of a sudden the peaks at the head of the valley, having been hidden for a while, become more intimate. A footbridge over a spectacular gorge allows an easier crossing than the early travellers had. No doubt this feature of the landscape was mentioned in the Maori traditions and songs that described the route.

Climb the terrace on the far side of the river to Mid Caples Hut, a small hut that has an enviable north-facing position looking up the valley.

In front of the hut is a textbook series of river terraces. At least four are visible. Since the end of the last ice age, the water weaving down the valley has varied in intensity. The rivers cut into the banks and when the river level subsides during a different climatic epoch, a new bank is cut, stranding the previous terrace up high.

Mid Caples Hut to Upper Caples Hut
2 hours ■ 6 km

Back on the track, a glance towards the hut reveals the resistant outcrop of rock bisecting the valley, the reason for the canyon before the hut. *Trentepohlia*, a red-coloured alga, coats the rocks of both tributary

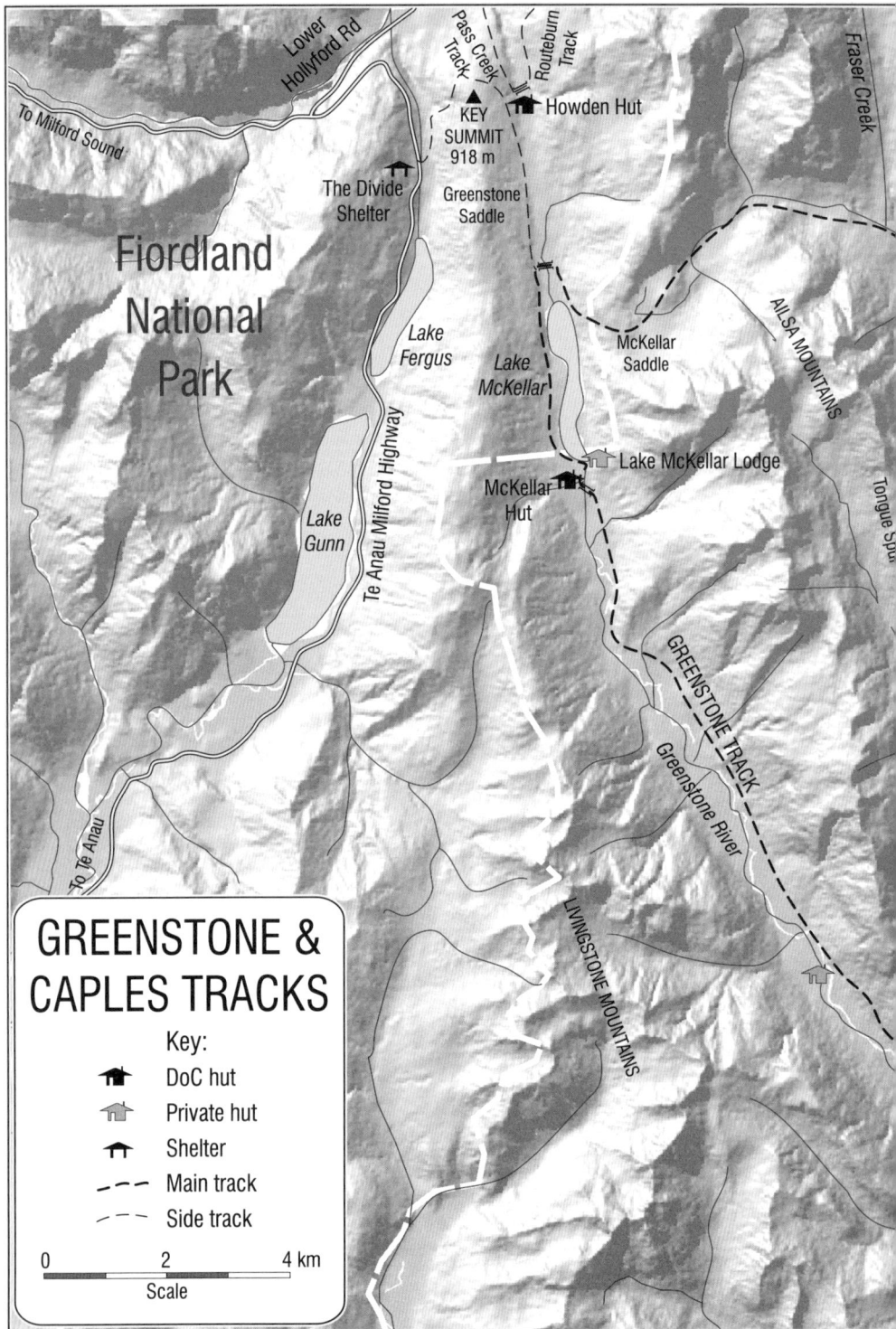

To Milford Sound

Lower Hollyford Rd

Pass Creek Track

Routeburn Track

Howden Hut

KEY SUMMIT 918 m

The Divide Shelter

Greenstone Saddle

Fiordland National Park

Fraser Creek

Lake Fergus

Lake McKellar

McKellar Saddle

AILSA MOUNTAINS

Te Anau Milford Highway

Lake McKellar Lodge

McKellar Hut

Lake Gunn

Tongue Spur

GREENSTONE TRACK

Greenstone River

To Te Anau

LIVINGSTONE MOUNTAINS

GREENSTONE & CAPLES TRACKS

Key:

🏠 DoC hut

🏠 Private hut

🏠 Shelter

--- Main track

- - - Side track

0   2   4 km

Scale

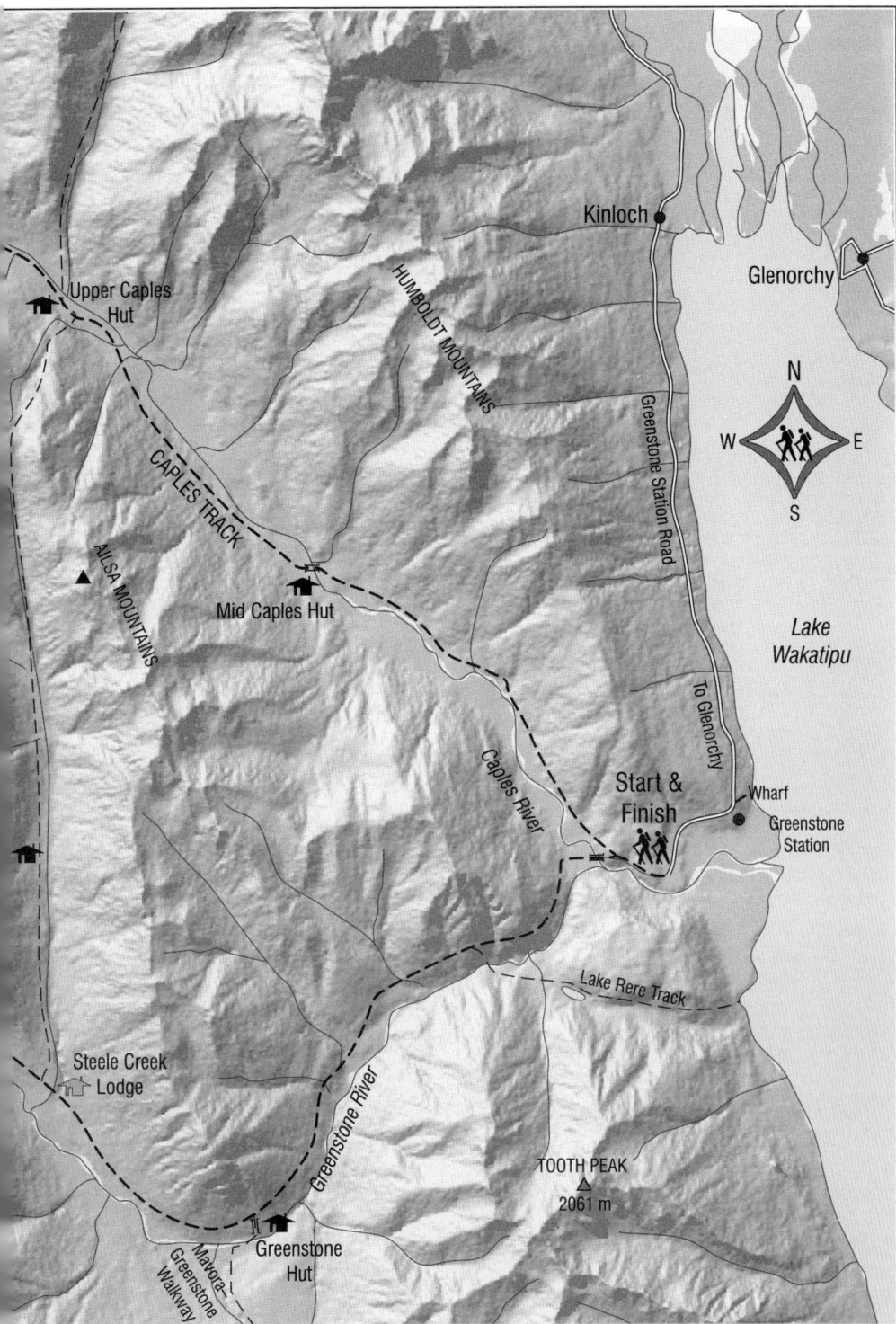

streams and the main river. The track again follows the bush edge, alternating between grassy clearings and forest. One clearing on the highest terrace seems to be surrounded on four sides by mountains.

The domination of beech is only once broken with a small collection of mountain toatoa, a *Phyllocladus* species with flattened stems in place of true leaves. The white timber is straight-grained, of considerable strength and dense. Maori extracted a red dye from the tannin-rich bark.

After a grassy enclave in the forest, at a sweep of the river, there are views to Mt Bonpland (2343 m) on the right. The track enters red beech forest. The saplings are uniform in height. Some track sections pass through corridors of seedlings densely smothering the forest floor. Galls – swellings of the plant tissue – encrust the many specimens and set the imagination working on what they resemble.

Kakariki, both yellow- and red-fronted, travel through the forest in flocks. Perhaps they are a spillover from the Eglinton Valley, where extensive predator control work has been carried out to preserve habitat for short-tailed bats and yellowheads.

A final stream crossing by a fallen mossy log leads to a clearing and Upper Caples Hut, dwarfed by Tongue Spur.

DAY TWO

Upper Caples Hut to McKellar Saddle
3 hours ■ 9.5 km

From the hut, pass by the footbridge over the river – this leads to Key Creek and Fraser Creek. Instead continue on the main Caples Valley track through red beech forest that soon becomes draped in cloaks of moss. Such is the coverage on all upward-facing surfaces, it looks as if the moss has fallen from the sky like snow. Riflemen, kakariki and robins hunt for insects, their calls mingling with the sounds of the Caples River.

Soon it's *au revoir* to the river for a while, as the track begins a gentle ascent. The going gets very rough, with numerous roots, rocks and muddy hollows, mulched up by a thousand passing trampers. Keep an eye out for track markers as sometimes the route is less than obvious. Riflemen explore the forest floor for titbits and probe bark for grubs.

On rejoining the Caples River, the track begins a steeper ascent. This is a world of large mossy boulders, gushing streams and clear water holes. Silver beech is the dominant tree, the canopy height lowering as you near the saddle. In heavy rain this area may become impassable as the dry creek may become a raging torrent. This is a sizeable catchment and the size of the boulders is testimony to the power the water can attain.

The transition to alpine flora is sudden. The silver beech is stunted and, here on the flats around the saddle, part of a mosaic of tarns and hardy shrubs. Hebes, some in whipcord form, are here with *Chionochloa spiralis* tussock and *Dracophyllum uniflorum*. Boardwalks protect the fragile flora. The faint click of landing grasshoppers and crickets echoes on the timber, almost at the limits of audibility.

McKellar Saddle to Caples/ Greenstone track junction
1 hour ■ 2 km

Passing over McKellar Saddle (945 m) the peaks of the Humboldts drift away behind, but a real treat lies ahead. Peeking over the ridge to the right, behind a silhouette of silver beech, is the pyramidal top of Mt Christina (2474 m). Then, as you wind down the boardwalk to begin the descent into the Greenstone Valley, she appears in her full glory. This is the best view of the elegant mountain and, such is the symmetry, you could be forgiven for thinking it was Mt Aspiring. Mt Crosscut (2263 m) comes into view as you re-enter the forest and descend.

The track doesn't bother with zigzags and traverses. It's straight down the hill and it's ugly stuff. There are large steps, numerous snaking roots and slippery rocks. If you find a flat spot to place a foot you are doing well, and in a few places you may need to reverse. A few glimpses of Lake McKellar appear through the foliage, but these are the only distraction. Concentrate and try to find a rhythm. The descent takes around 1 hour.

After the descent there is a long traverse with a few streams and bogs to cross. Eventually the track exits onto grassland at the head of the Greenstone River and meets the Greenstone Track.

If you started at the Divide, head right to return there. It will take you around 2½ hours.

Caples/ Greenstone track junction to McKellar Hut
1 hour ■ 3 km

After the bridge, turn left down the Greenstone Valley. The few boggy patches on the track shouldn't trouble leather boots and gaiters. As the track skirts Lake McKellar it dives in and out of the forest and crosses several creeks. Approaching the tail end of the lake, trampers have worn a couple of tracks that duck down to the inviting shingle beaches on the shore. There's the opportunity for a dip in the meltwater if you're game.

Shortly after, the track exits Fiordland National Park and enters the Greenstone Conservation Area, but the magnificence of the setting alters little. McKellar Hut sits in a clearing by the Greenstone River under the watch of 2000 m peaks.

DAY THREE

McKellar Hut to Steele Creek

4 hours ■ 11 km

For the next hour the track swaps its route between the tussock flats and a bench in the forest-covered mountainside. There may be squelchy bits on the flat and the forest sections are a rocky, bouldery hotchpotch. The river rustles below. In the forest, compare this relatively sparse eastern beech forest with the wetter western forest encountered at the Divide.

As you leave the forest, you will come to a vantage point down the valley to where it veers sharp left. It has the U-shaped profile characteristic of valleys carved out by glaciers. Follow the orange marker posts over the grassy fan, which is the consolidated terminal face of a scree slope. There's the odd pocket of forest, but for most of the next 30 minutes you'll be in the open with kea for company. The forest edge is clear cut, with only the occasional daring – but pathetically spindly – silver beech seeming to make a dash from its comrades to join the shrubby coprosmas.

On the ground in the forest pockets there is a thatch of fallen silver beech twigs. The trees rid themselves of decaying appendages without risking invasion by fungi and insects by gently squeezing the twig off the parent branch. When the wind blows the twig off the branch, instead of leaving a large open wound it leaves a small hole in the bark. This process is known as abscission.

Cross a couple of footbridges in quick succession, the first of them over a photogenic rushing stream. Over the next 2 hours the character of the forest changes. The silver beech canopy to start with is relatively low and, save the odd prickly shield fern and moss, nothing grows below. An entry way of mountain toatoa and tree fuchsia announces a transition to red beech forest. It feels different in here. The

Coprosma, a woody divaricating shrub, is brutal stuff to browse if you're a ground-dwelling bird such as a moa. It is thought this is one reason so many New Zealand shrubs have this growth form – a deterrent to being munched. The meagre foliage wouldn't even pass for a canapé, while the twigs would have poked the moa's eyes if it ventured any deeper than the outermost layer.

canopy is higher, the trunks more substantial and an understorey of seedlings flourishes. The silver and red beech forests then interchange, possibly in response to variations in drainage patterns – red beech prefers drier soils and tends to occur on steeper slopes with a more rubbly base and less developed soils. Riflemen, with their barely audible cheeps, flit about.

The track has a rocky section where it crosses an old land slip. A few hardy specimens of silver beech have colonised this barren surface, but it will be a few thousand years before it reverts to forest. The break in the forest allows for a view up the valley, where Mt Christina pokes her summit above the tops of the Livingstone Mountains. The rocky line near the mountain tops indicates the height of the last glacier.

Staying close to the river, you will soon come out on to a flat, where the dense combs of tussock gyrate in the breeze. The track is sometimes squelchy, but the odd bit of boardwalk and rocky sections provide a firmer footing. The view down the valley to the junction with the head of the Mararoa Valley and the peaks behind is enticing.

The track passes an elevated rocky section, one side rounded smooth and of gentle contour and the other steeper and craggier. This is a *roche moutonnée* shaped by glaciation. Bog pine carpets the valley floor on the approach to the junction with Steele Creek.

The swingbridge over Steele Creek is not for those who suffer from vertigo – at one time a huge volume of water must have streamed out of the watershed to incise a gorge so deep. When a river encounters a resistant outcrop it is channelled into any weakness in the rock. This constriction funnels the erosive power down and a chasm is formed.

Steele Creek to Greenstone Hut
2 hours ▪ 6 km

The track soon drops into the bed of the former river. In post-glacial times the water locked up in the body of the glaciers melted and formed torrid flows that eroded away the debris the glacier had left behind. The sculpted moraines on these sections of the track form a series of terraces, indicating different water levels.

The track is good going, flat and well-drained. As it begins to skirt the base of the range it enters mountain beech forest. Myriad matchstick trunks give the forest a haunted feel – it feels like you are inside a Francis Bacon or Edvard Munch painting.

The route follows the edge of the rounded tail of the Ailsa Range until a signpost indicates the Greenstone Hut, your destination today.

Cross the footbridge over the gorge and the hut soon appears. The hut is well sited in a clearing with views in both directions, and it laps up the evening sun.

DAY FOUR

Greenstone Hut to Greenstone/ Caples track junction

2 hours ■ 8 km

Retrace your steps over the swingbridge to the Greenstone Track and turn right. The track passes through forest of red beech, mountain beech, or a mixture, according to soil, aspect and drainage. After 1 hour, cross Slip Creek, either at the mouth or if the water level is high via the emergency bridge. The flats give open views down the valley to the confluence of Greenstone and Caples Rivers.

It's back into the forest, passing a set of waterfalls. The first is low and voluminous with a big rock at its base. The next two are silvery threads edged with mossy borders. Pass the junction (1 hour) with the track to Lake Rere before exiting onto the expansive grassy flats at the bottom of the Caples Valley. A last look back up the Greenstone gives a view of Tooth Peak with a foreground of divaricating matagouri. The scene is a bucolic idyll.

Descend to the footbridge over the Caples River and the junction with the Caples Track. If you have started at the Divide, turn left onto the Caples – unless you want to make the detour to Lake Wakatipu.

Greenstone/ Caples track junction to Greenstone road end

30 min ■ 2 km

If you started the tramp at the end of Greenstone Station Road, head right over that final undulation back towards Lake Wakatipu. This is where early travellers with their greenstone treasures would have linked up with a waiting waka to transport them to the Clutha River system. It's a poignant spot to reflect on the journeys made by these bold explorers. Their connection with the land and knowledge of the route and its features represented a way of life now lost.

REES–DART TRACK

73 km (including Cascade Saddle) ■ five days ■ one way

The Rees–Dart Track, although located mostly within Mount Aspiring National Park, has much in common with its Fiordland counterparts, including the glacial landforms, the alpine and valley plants – and the awe-inspiring scenery. The walk travels along two valleys linked by a saddle. The Rees and Dart Valleys have distinct characteristics, but the Dart is marginally more spectacular because of the glacier views in the Snowdrift and Barrier Ranges. A must-do side trip for the tramp is to Cascade Saddle, making the four-day tramp into a five-day outing. The tramping surface is quite rough and the ascent of Rees and Cascade Saddles makes it physically demanding.

On day one the track follows the wide open Rees Valley in the shadow of Mt Earnslaw/Pikirakatahi. This dominant mountain rises more than 2 km above the grassy flats. Day two begins with a climb up to the Rees Saddle and the broken rocks of the upper watershed. Descending via Snowy Creek you will get the first glimpse of the glaciers that are a highlight of the walk. The steep watercourse is crossed by dramatic bridges with attractive stream boulders below.

Day three is taken up by a side trip to Cascade Saddle, with a choice of scenes – the Dart Glacier or the highest peaks of Mount Aspiring National Park, including Aspiring herself. The retreating Dart Glacier offers a lesson in geomorphology. Day four descends the Dart Valley, crossing open flats and beech forest sections. The milky waters of the river and jumble of boulders provide many tranquil interludes. Day five continues down the Dart River past the glaciers of the Barrier Range to the road end at Chinamans Bluff.

Long before European exploration, South Island Maori were using the mouth of the Dart River as a stopping-off point in their search for pounamu. Archaeological remains from the 14th century include a series of mounds that indicate the structure of early dwellings. Slab-paved pathways connected the rudimentary houses and drainage ditches controlled water flows. The site is also significant for the flaked hammer-dressed Routeburn greenstone found there, along with middens containing moa bones.

Permanent Maori settlement of inland Otago took place from the late 18th century. Controlled burning cleared land around the Rees and the Dart for cultivating potatoes. A further archaeological site on Camp Hill by the Rees was inhabited in the early 19th century by Ngai Tahu, who had displaced Ngati Mamoe and Waitaha from the region. The defended site probably controlled access to greenstone sources in both the Dart catchment and Fiordland.

Following the 1861 discovery of gold at Tuapeka, prospectors poured in to Otago from the Victorian goldfields. To the embarrassment of the survey department, there had been no accurate survey of the inland Otago regions, and district surveyor John Turnbull Thompson appointed a young Scot, James McKerrow, to fill in the map. McKerrow pursued his brief with gusto and determination. In February 1863, he and his party ascended Mt Nicholas west of Lake Wakatipu, rowed to the mouth of the Greenstone River, climbed Mt Alfred near the mouth of the Rees River, and followed the Rees 35 km from Lake Wakatipu to near the Rees Saddle. They explored the Dart Valley, encountering numerous gold diggers and prospectors on the way. Early runholder W. G. Rees had in 1860 set up a sheep station at the head of Lake Wakatipu between the Rees and Dart Valleys.

The explorations of the other valleys were undertaken by early prospectors who closely guarded their knowledge. Among other adventurers in the region, Patrick Quirk Caples also explored the Rees

SECTION TIMINGS

DAY ONE 7 hours 17.5 km

Muddy Creek to Twenty-Five Mile Creek	2¼ hours	6.5 km
Twenty-Five Mile Creek to Slip Flat	3 hours	6.5 km
Slip Flat to Shelter Rock Hut	1¾ hours	4.5 km

DAY TWO 5 hours 9 km

Shelter Rock Hut to Rees Saddle	2½ hours	4 km
Rees Saddle to Dart Hut	2½ hours	5 km

DAY THREE 7 hours 16 km

Cascade Saddle (optional)	7 hours	16 km return

DAY FOUR 5½ hours 15.5 km

Dart Hut to Cattle Flat	3 hours	8.5 km
Cattle Flat to Daleys Flat Hut	2½ hours	7 km

DAY FIVE 5 hours 15 km

Daleys Flat Hut to Sandy Bluff	1¾ hours	6 km
Sandy Bluff to Chinamans car park	3 hours	9 km

Valley. He is said to have made the first record of the Dart Glacier, describing it as 'a very large glacier surrounded by perpendicular mountains'. He also named Snowy Creek. The Dart Valley was not properly surveyed until James Park undertook the work in 1886.

Fifty years of mountaineering completed the human discoveries of the region. One of the most notable peaks was Mt Earnslaw/Pikirakatahi. The East Peak was bagged in 1890 by Harry Birley but the West Peak was not climbed until 1914. By the late 1920s interest in the region spiralled with the formation of the Otago Section of the NZ Alpine Club (OSONZAC) and by 1938 all the major peaks had been climbed.

The Rees–Dart Track is a loop around Mt Earnslaw/Pikirakatahi and the Forbes Range. Glenorchy has traditionally been the departure point for exploration of the region, but until 1962 when the road from Queenstown was finally completed, the main access was by steamer, including the *Earnslaw*.

BOOKING

The Rees–Dart Track is not a Great Walk, so beds are available on a first-come first-served basis. You must purchase hut tickets in advance from DoC centres. There are three huts (Shelter Rock Hut 22 bunks, Dart Hut 32 bunks, Daleys Flat Hut 20 bunks). None has gas, so you'll need to bring your own stove. Camping is permitted anywhere except in the fragile alpine and subalpine areas between Shelter Rock Hut and Dart Hut. Camping is not permitted on Cascade Saddle itself. There is no fee for camping unless hut facilities are used.

Terralink's Aspiring & Rees/Dart Recreation Areas map is the best.

GETTING THERE

It is best to take a shuttle rather than your own vehicle. Getting between the road ends is a pain, as they are some distance apart and the Rees end sees little traffic so you may find it hard to get a lift.

From November to April, Info & Track runs a daily shuttle departing 37 Shotover Street, Queenstown at 8 am, arriving Glenorchy at 9 am and at Muddy Creek on the Rees at 10 am. The return service departs Chinamans Bluff on the Dart at 2 pm, arriving in Glenorchy 30 minutes later and connecting with a bus to Queenstown, arriving at 4 pm. Reservations are essential.

Info & Track
0-3-442 9708
www.infotrack.co.nz

DAY ONE

Muddy Creek to Twenty-Five Mile Creek
2¼ hours ■ 6.5 km

The start of the track follows a four-wheel-drive road, which winds up the true left of the river. Several creeks cross the track, while on the flats marker poles show the way around the poorly drained patches. Occasional forays up the valley side, the most lofty after around 1½ hours, give a chance to take in the surroundings – grassy flats, the braided Rees River, and a few well-weathered farm buildings hugging the valley edge. Thorny trackside matagouri scrapes your legs occasionally.

The Earnslaw Glacier tumbles off the south-eastern face of Mt Earnslaw/Pikirakatahi (2830 m) to the left. Ahead there are some notable river terraces deposited during the glacier's retreat. The Forbes Mountains, Mt Clarke (2285 m), The Osonzac Twins (2282 m) and Moira Peak (2495 m) stand out, all with glaciers hanging off their southern faces. Light shafts play on the mountainsides and passing showers form the sun's rays into dynamic light shows.

It's around 45 minutes further to Twenty-Five Mile Creek. Follow the creek a few minutes past the rock bivvy to a narrow gorge in which the rushing waters echo. In the shaded light the water is utterly clear and tinged with a soft blue light.

Twenty-Five Mile Creek to Slip Flat
3 hours ■ 6.5 km

Unless you're wearing very tight gaiters you will get wet feet crossing Twenty-Five Mile Creek, which can rise rapidly in flood. A nearby plaque notes that two unfortunate trampers drowned here – if the level is high, shelter in the bivvy and wait for the waters to subside. Over the next rise is a perfect rock bivvy for one. It overlooks the valley, Lennox Falls and Mt Earnslaw/Pikirakatahi.

The track follows the braided river, through occasional pockets of mountain beech. As you round the river terrace there are views further up the valley. The jagged mudstone bluffs high on the right line the ridge like a military battalion but look perilously unstable. The bush-edge trees drip old man's beard, a lichen that smothers some trees completely.

After 1 hour the track enters mountain and silver beech forest with a sparse understorey of prickly shield fern, and dense carpets of moss and filmy ferns beneath. Around 15 minutes later, cross the swingbridge and enter Mount Aspiring National Park. Traversing the valley edge, the track now climbs steadily. A mix of mountain and silver beech overtops the mossy forest floor, where the greens are almost luminous. Slip Flat is the clearing beyond the great Clarke Slip.

Slip Flat to Shelter Rock Hut
1¾ hours ■ 4.5 km

On the far side of the valley, a slip has brought down tonnes of debris and killed the surrounding trees. It must have originally dammed the river. If you take a plate of rock from the weathered trackside boulders you will find it crumbles in your finger like talcum powder. The mica sparkles as if deposited by the dust of a moth's wings.

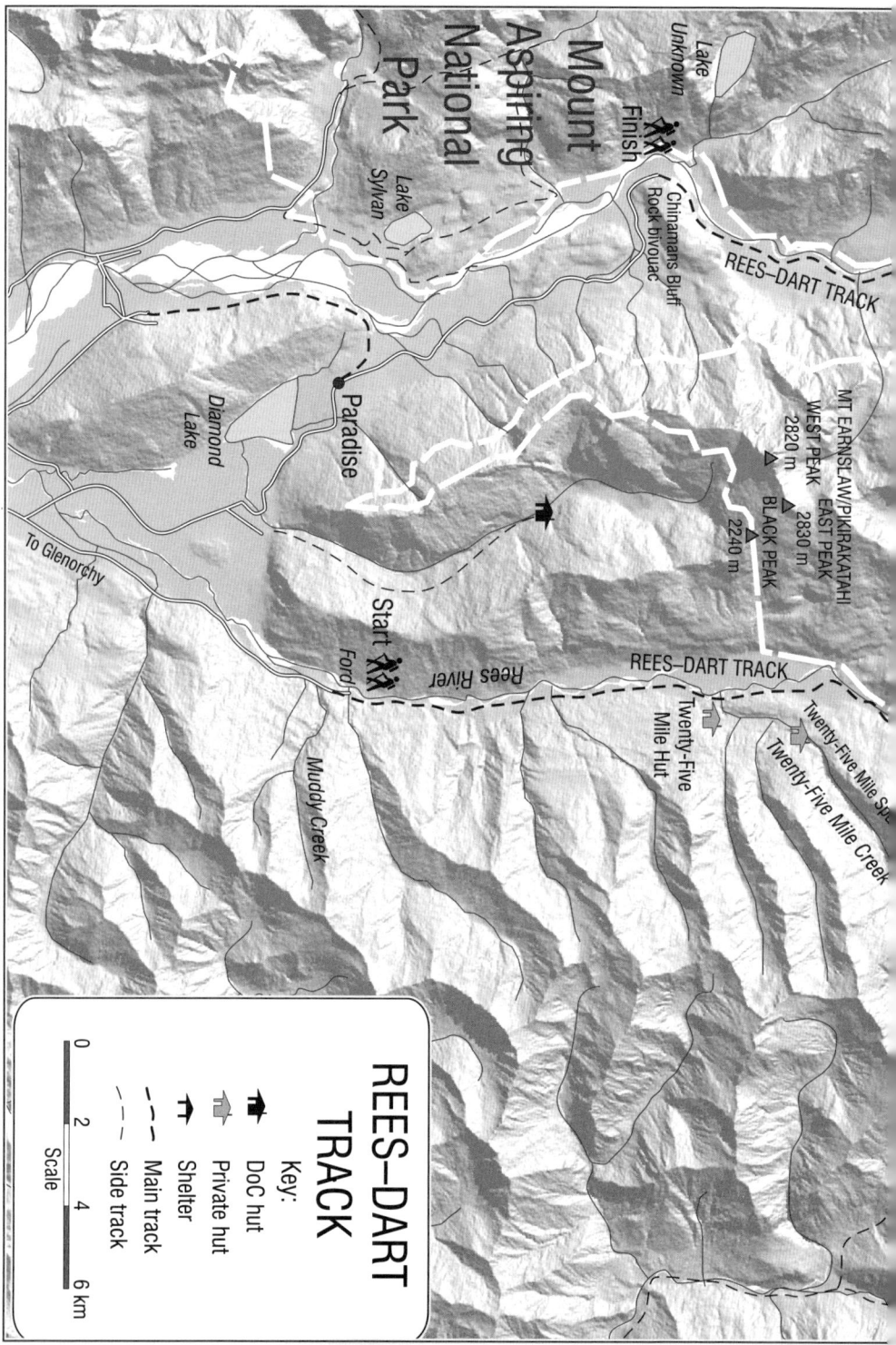

REES–DART TRACK

Key:

🏚	DoC hut
🏚	Private hut
➡	Shelter
— — —	Main track
- - -	Side track

Scale
0   2   4   6 km

Mount Aspiring National Park

Lake Unknown

Finish

Lake Sylvan

Chinamans Bluff
Rock bivouac

REES–DART TRACK

Diamond Lake

Paradise

To Glenorchy

MT EARNSLAW/PIKIRAKATAHI
WEST PEAK 2820 m
EAST PEAK 2830 m
BLACK PEAK 2240 m

Start
Ford
Rees River

REES–DART TRACK

Twenty-Five Mile Hut
Twenty-Five Mile Creek
Twenty-Five Mile Spur

Muddy Creek

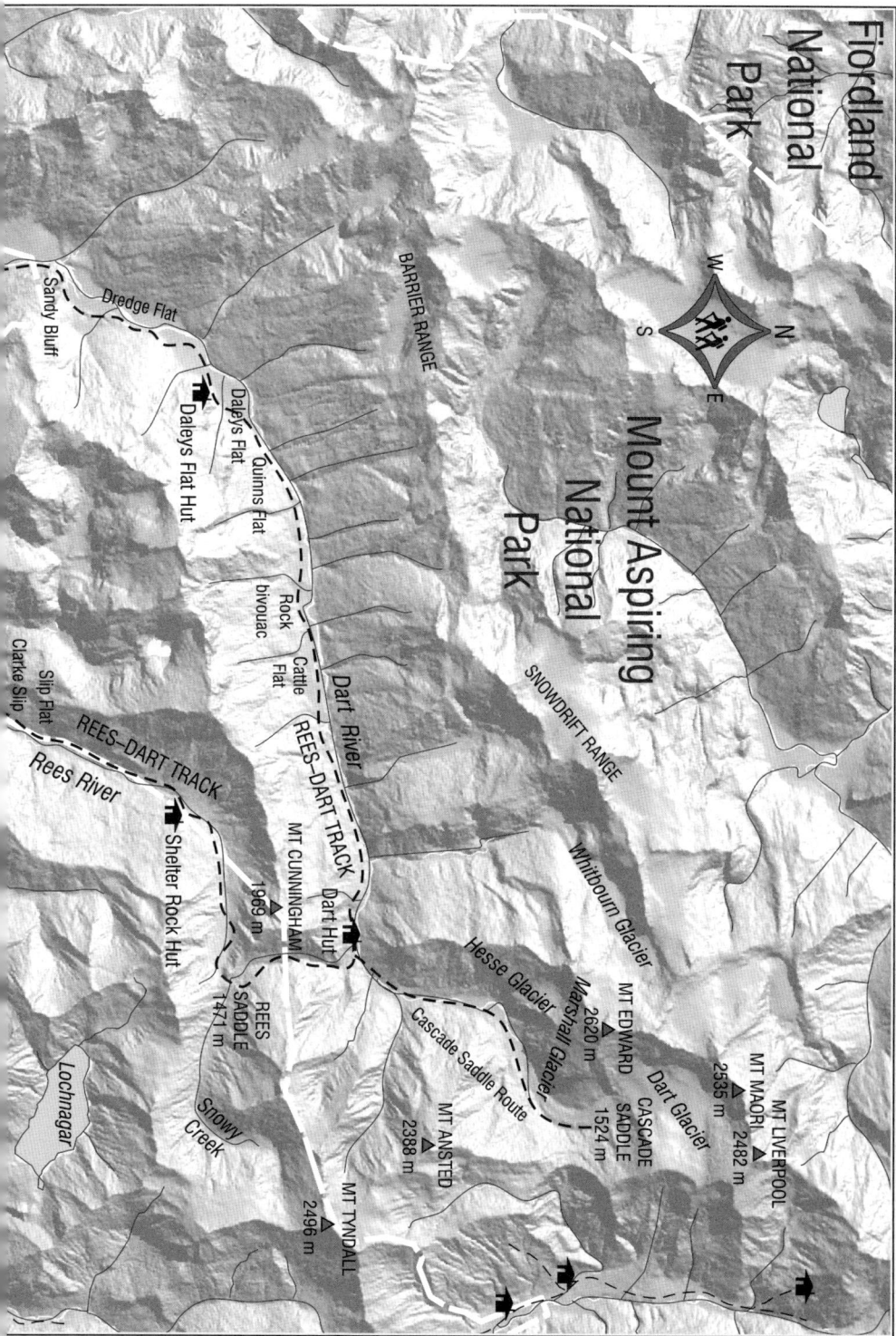

Back in the forest, beyond a glade of mountain ribbonwood, the track can be muddy. A pretty waterfall, white water veins encircling mossy boulders, is followed by another higher fall. Some large boulders have peeled off the higher slopes and found temporary residence in the forest. Two have formed a triangular tunnel. When you leave the forest, signs warn you are about to cross the path of avalanches that in spring and early summer fall off the upper slopes of Mt Clarke and lumber down the gullies. There's a reason no forest grows here.

The rock faces at the head of the valley have steeply inclined bedding planes. Where end grains are exposed at the ridge, the jagged series of outcrops resemble a toothed saw. As the track continues uphill, alpine vegetation surreptitiously takes over with speargrass, mountain toatoa, hebes, *Dracophyllum uniflorum* and *D. longifolium* forming intricate gardens. It's not long before Shelter Rock Hut appears on the far side of the valley, reached by a swingbridge.

DAY TWO

Shelter Rock Hut to Rees Saddle
2½ hours ■ 4 km

The Rees River must attain some volume to churn up the wide river bed, despite the fact it is high up the watershed. A series of cairns leads you up the river, passing interesting boulders encrusted with a mosaic of cushion mosses, *Trentepohlia* algae and lichens.

Fairly soon the track cuts above the river and starts the steady climb to the saddle. Mt Earnslaw/Pikirakatahi peeks from the skyline behind, but is soon obscured by the ridge of Mt Clarke. The alpine gardens feature broad-leaved snow tussock, pygmy pine and whipcord hebes. Watch out for the giant speargrass, as it can grate your legs.

The final climb to the saddle is steep and follows poles below a rock buttress. Although mostly mud-derived rock, the ridge also shows up lenses of green-tinged sandstone, which is more common around the Humboldt Mountains and Serpentine Range near the Routeburn. Kea fly between the valley sides, shrieking. The uncommon New Zealand pipit chits around, a bird seemingly too delicate for its harsh surroundings. Crickets and moths provide food for the birds.

Rees Saddle (1471 m), where there is not a single tree amid the tussock grassland, really feels like the mountains. Glaciers on the peaks to the north include the Hobbs Glacier below Marion Tower (2343 m) and the upper part of the Whitbourn Glacier. Smooth rock faces to the east have been glacially scoured along the bedding planes and look like rhino hide. Take a short walk up from the pass for views down the Rees Valley.

The descent from the saddle is much steeper than the ascent and threads a fine course through fields of snow tussock. Up the valley there is a mass of smoothed rock and scree but there are views down the valley of the gorge-like Snowy Creek and distant Mt Edward (2620 m). Glaciers drape off the southern faces, with the tongue-like Hesse Glacier penetrating down a gully towards the Dart Valley floor. This scene continuously changes on the descent, and is only briefly obscured when you cross the Snowy Creek swingbridge.

Rees Saddle to Dart Hut
2½ hours ■ 5 km

Even in summer, it takes no great leap of imagination to see that the steep smooth valley walls are avalanche zones. Early in the walking season this section can be a death trap, so heed any warnings from DoC before setting out. The swingbridge is removed in winter, making this section more dangerous, especially when snowmelt raises the river level.

As the descent continues, the Snowdrift Range and Mt Lydia (2517 m) appear further down the Dart Valley, with the Ferrier Glacier beneath the summit ridge. The track goes steeply down the spur towards the Dart Hut, which you will come to after crossing a second swingbridge. The fancy new hut with a big deck is in a sunny spot overlooked by Mt Anstead (2388 m).

DAY THREE

Before contemplating this side trip, you need to know about safety issues. The poled alpine route is a fine-weather tramp only. There are no views in the rain anyway. Snow makes the track treacherous – there is avalanche danger from June to November and cold snaps can bring

Cascade Saddle
7 hours ■ 16 km return

snow any time of year. Side creeks can flood in rain. Do not attempt this route in anything except fine weather.

From the Dart Hut, cross the swingbridge and traverse the toe of the spur. The larger creeks should not be attempted in wet weather. Early or late in the walking season, the heath plants on the valley floor are encrusted with ice. Right from the start, you will get a sense of this wild and dynamic environment. Views of the Hesse Glacier, with its ice towers and crevassed flow, are overshadowed by the Marshall Glacier below Mt Edward, pristine white in comparison.

Cross the two rocky protrusions into the valley floor, the first long and gradual, the second short and steep. As you round a corner in the Dart River you will get your first look at Cascade Saddle and the glacial country really begins. This next section is a mobile lesson in geomorphology.

> The valley floor is completely filled with moraine, a mass of unrounded, unsorted debris in all sizes from silt to boulders as big as trucks. The perfect circular hollows are sink holes created by ice pieces swamped with rock debris melting into their holes. The rock piles in the centre of the valley are abandoned lumps of glacier hidden within moraine, and on the far side of the valley are pieces of ice from the edge of the retreating glacier.

The track nips into a gut and passes a lake of gin-clear water, then begins the main ascent above the snout of the Dart Glacier. With the climb, the views of the glacier are ever-changing. Lines of moraine, crevasses and the snaking tongue of the glacier lead up to seracs and ice towers below its plateau. The ridge above the glacier is peppered by peaks – Maoriri, Maruiwi, Maiti-iti, Maori, Wahine – with Pakeha Col between these last two.

The track traverses steep scree, sometimes inducing the typical 'two steps forward one step back' routine. Side creeks have excavated deep gullies, which can be challenging to get down and out of – it can be a bit of a scramble. Your attention may be grabbed by the scary sound of rockfall or avalanches on the far side of the valley, the faces which take the morning sun.

The view up to the Dart Glacier keeps getting better – it may be hard to find a rhythm because you keep looking at the view. This glacier was surveyed in 1914, by a party headed by F. B. Leonard, but today its snout is about 3 km further up the valley from where it is on the first map. The current rate of retreat is estimated at 50 m per year. The saddle itself was first crossed, from the Matukituki side, in 1911 by Bernard Head.

Kea live here as wild birds, free from the scrounging habits of others in more touristy spots. They forage in the snowgrass, turning up turf in search of insects and grubs. The track heads straight, following the hollow behind a kame terrace. A rockery of boulders frames the view up the Dart Glacier before the final ascent to the saddle.

The views from Cascade Saddle are astounding. On the Matukituki side a new set of mountains comes to light, including Mt Aspiring (3033 m), Mt Avalanche (2606 m) and Rob Roy Peak (2644 m). Sidle up the ridge and views of Aspiring become clearer. You can even make out French Ridge Hut and the profile of Coxcomb Ridge. Head down to the saddle proper to get a view of the cliff face and the reason behind the name of Cascade Saddle. A giant waterfall leaps down the near-vertical face, its notes echoing off the walls of the bowl.

The seracs on the Dart Glacier, tumbling over the sill at the base of the ice plateau, glow blue as the sun lights them from behind. The crevasses on the outside corner are like knife gouges on the ice field. Listen for the creaks of ice, sounding like an unoiled wooden door.

There is a legitimate campsite near the saddle on a plateau just below the main ridge. This would be a memorable spot to see sunrise and sunset, but not the place to be in a storm. The descent gives time to examine the efforts of DoC rangers and passing trampers, who have left a legacy of cairn art throughout the valley. Frequently topped with pure quartz, the cairns have been carefully designed to showcase the best rock samples. Many of them are of human height and they stand out like beacons. Less carefully arranged rock piles atop boulders probably contain the annual count of passing trampers.

DAY FOUR

Follow the benched track below the hut, passing through open silver and mountain beech forest with a light leaf litter and an understorey of prickly shield fern, saplings and mosses. There are many toppled trees, victims of beech's shallow radial root system. This large volume of decaying wood provides nutrients for the next generation as fungi and bacteria break the wood down to its constituent minerals.

Dart Hut to Cattle Flat
3 hours ■ 8.5 km

On the opposite bank of the Dart River there are a couple of large slips that occasionally release boulders into the river with a thunderous crash. Pretty side creeks cross the track, a trend abruptly terminated on the exit from the forest after about 2 hours.

Here you come across one of the side creeks you are warned not to cross in heavy rain. In benign conditions the flow is a trickle, but the 5 m high bank on the far side is all the evidence you need to understand the force the water can have. Cross the fan at the mouth of the creek onto the grassy flats, with views of the Barrier Range and glacial ice towers resembling castle battlements. Three river terraces are stepped into the valley floor downstream. The track undulates between the gullies.

After 45 minutes there's a short steep rise into the forest before the track reaches into the grassy clearing where a footbridge over the Dart gives mountaineers access to the Barrier Range. A sign announcing Cattle Flat is a few minutes from a rock bivvy at the edge of the forest.

Cattle Flat to Daleys Flat Hut
2½ hours ■ 7 km

Out in the open of the valley floor now, you can tick off the glaciers as they pass – the Key Dome, Blue Duck, Hamilton and Curzon. East of O'Leary Pass, named after Arawata Bill O'Leary, is the Barrier Range, with the Chancellor and Abruzzi Glaciers.

Re-enter the forest 45 minutes after Cattle Flat. The conspicuous delicate fern fringing the track is thousand-leaved fern. It is joined by beds of lycopods, moss relatives that were the predominant plant type when dinosaurs roamed in Jurassic times. In late summer and early autumn, brightly coloured fungi abound.

Quinns Flat, a brief grassy interlude before you re-enter the forest, is an hour on. Daleys Flat is at the far end of the next clearing, with another footbridge close by. Below the bridge the river is so choked with glacial rock flour its colour resembles the bill of a whio.

Daleys Flat Hut is at the edge of the forest with a view up the river. It's a nice spot. The sandflies think so too.

DAY FIVE

Daleys Flat Hut to Sandy Bluff
1¾ hours ■ 6 km

Follow the track through red beech forest that is more open and airy than the silver and mountain beech forests of yesterday. The first clearing is known as Dredge Flat, after the gold dredge that worked here between 1899 and 1902. The remains of the pontoon are at the upper end.

Back in the forest there are occasional views framed by the foliage. At the next clearing a large bluff to the left shows the cross section of the stratified river debris transported during times of higher flow. In the distance the dead trees of a big slip are now a ghostly forest of spires. Sandy Bluff is a visual cue to see how far you have to walk.

The track around the steep bluff has been blasted into the rock face and a handrail has been bolted onto the rock. Watch out for rockfalls during rain and concentrate – it's a 70 m drop.

Sandy Bluff to Chinamans car park
3 hours ▪ 9 km

At the base of the bluff there is another small clearing before the track enters more forest, occasionally dipping to the river. Massive boulders capped with silver beech trees obstruct the flow. Other river sections are braided, a sign that the river is now lower in its course.

Bird life has become more prolific here since Operation Ark has reduced predator numbers, creating a safer haven for endangered species such as yellowheads and kakariki. Even in the dark red beech forest the yellowheads stand out, while the excited chatter of kakariki fills the air as they remove bark to glean grubs. Totara enters the forest mix, along with ground ferns, horopito and stinkwood (one of the coprosmas), a sign the altitude is lower and temperatures are warmer.

As you exit the final clearing Chinamans Bluff towers above. The parched flats look up the Beans Burn, the Dart now concealed behind the bluff. A few lone beech trees survive on the valley floor, but otherwise the flat bottom is only grass. Sidle around the final section of the bluff to the car park.

FURTHER READING

Books about Fiordland are sought-after treasures. There is a group of passionate collectors out there who will pay exorbitant prices for rare and collectible volumes. I know this because I have become one!

Most of the titles listed are available in Te Anau or Queenstown, but the best place to buy Fiordland books is at Gunns Camp on the Hollyford Road. For rarer titles, get onto Google and get out the credit card.

General

Department of Lands and Survey. *The Story of Fiordland National Park.* Fiordland National Park Board, 1986.

A basic introduction to the national park. Chapters on the geology, forest, animal life, pre-European and European histories give a background for exploration of the park. A good selection of colour pictures.

Geology

Graeme Stevens, Matt McGlone and Beverley McCulloch; illustrations by Vivian Ward. *Prehistoric New Zealand.* Heinemann Reed, Auckland, 1988.

This is the definitive narrative of New Zealand's geology, told like a story and giving a perspective for current debates on climate change. Lavishly illustrated with photographs and paintings, it also serves as a celebration of our indigenous fauna and landscapes.

Botany
Lawrie Metcalf. *A Photographic Guide to Ferns of New Zealand*. New Holland, 2003, and *A Photographic Guide to Alpine Plants of New Zealand*. New Holland, 2006.

These handy, pocket-size guides provide good descriptions of key identification features, and are illustrated with colour photographs throughout.

J. T. Salmon. *The Native Trees of New Zealand*. Reed, Auckland, 1980.

This is the bible of native trees. More than 1500 photos accompany notes on every tree in the country. This is one for collectors.

A. L. Poole. *Southern Beeches*. DSIR, Wellington, 1987.

An in-depth look at the southern beeches, their place in the New Zealand botanical story, and their distribution.

A. F. Mark and Nancy M. Adams. *New Zealand Alpine Plants*. Reed Methuen, Auckland, 1986 (2nd edition).

A compendium of alpine plants in New Zealand, with detailed descriptions, colour plates and gems about the derivation of names.

Natural history
Neville Peat. *Wild Fiordland*. University of Otago Press, Dunedin, 1996.

Peat writes about the natural history of the southern South Island with lively interest and compassion. He distils academic information into a readable book with all you need to know on the subject.

Conservation
Gerard Hutching and Craig Potton (editors). *Forests, Fiords and Glaciers: The Case for a South-West New Zealand World Heritage Site*. Royal Forest and Bird Protection Society of New Zealand, Wellington, 1987.

This volume successfully presented the case for World Heritage status being conferred on the south-west corner of New Zealand. With chapters on the geology, botany, fauna, human exploration and exploitation and the political context surrounding preservation, it is an essential read.

History

John Hall-Jones. *The Fjords of Fiordland*. Craig Printing, Invercargill, 2002.

This book has a great stock of black-and-white images that are poorly complemented with colour shots. Rather too much information is given on snippets of Fiordland history.

John Hall-Jones. *Fiordland Explored*. Reed, Wellington, 1976.

An overall historical volume on Fiordland, with reasonable levels of depth on all major locations and themes.

Marios Gavalas. *Fiordland, Southland and Stewart Island/Rakiura Landmarks*. Reed, Auckland, 2007.

Tramping

Mark Pickering. *A Tramper's Journey*. Craig Potton, Nelson, 2004.

After an exploration that has spanned three decades, Pickering has become the undisputed expert on New Zealand's backcountry. These stories together try to explain the motivations, experiences, camaraderie, skills and downright hardships of tramping. It is about the only book that does any justice to the question 'Why tramp?'

Shaun Barnett and Rob Brown. *Classic Tramping in New Zealand*. Craig Potton, Nelson, 1999.

The authors are widely travelled within New Zealand and give personal accounts of their trips, interspersed with snippets of history, anecdotes and tramping culture. The photos are breathtaking. The 12 tramps vary in difficulty and degree of renown.

Tuatapere Hump Ridge Track

Warren Bird. *Viaducts Against the Sky*. Craig Printing, Invercargill, 1998.

This is a detailed and fluidly written account of the complete Port Craig story. Well illustrated and full of quirky anecdotes about life in the sawmill.

Kepler Track

Jane Forsyth, Ian Turnbull, Bill Lee and Gary Beecroft. *A Guide to the Kepler Track*. McIndoe in association with DSIR, Dunedin, 1991.

An informative guide written by professional staff including geologists and botanists, bringing to light the natural history of the track.

Routeburn Track

Doreen McKenzie. *Road to Routeburn*. McIndoe, Dunedin, 1973.
A selection of tales from the pioneering days at the head of Lake Wakatipu and accounts of travels over the Routeburn Track.

Milford Track

John Hall-Jones. *Milford Sound*. Craig Printing, Invercargill, 2000.
A good, although at times exasperating, collection of historical snippets on the track, sound and road.

William Anderson. *Milford Trails*. Reed, Wellington, 1971.
Bill Anderson was a legendary hut warden, track worker and guide on the Milford. His love affair with the track spanned four decades. This is the finest collection of historical notes interwoven with personal anecdotes on New Zealand's most famous track.

Blanche E. Baughan. *The Finest Walk in the World*. Whitcombe & Tombs, Auckland, 1928 (4th edition).
The original poetic description of a walk down the Milford Track.

Hollyford Track

Gordon Donaldson-Law. *Hollyford Muster*. S. D. Donaldson-Law, Nelson, 1995.
Donaldson-Law accompanied Davey Gunn on a series of musters in the Hollyford, Kaipo and Big Bay areas in 1948. Here, in surprisingly eloquent style, free from the stuffiness often pervading literature of the day, Law describes the hardships and technical details of months spent mustering in this untracked vastness.

Rupert Sharpe. *Fiordland Muster*. Hodder & Stoughton, London, 1966.
Sharpe, like Law, accompanied Gunn on a muster on the Hollyford. A writer for the *Daily News*, Sharpe was an accomplished outdoorsman who enjoyed a good fish and hunt. His lively account gives an insight into Davey Gunn's nature and personality, notwithstanding a few niggles at some of his employer's habits and styles. The descriptions of the scenery are almost poetic in places.

Alice McKenzie. *The Pioneers of Martins Bay*. Lakes District Museum in association with Alice Margaret Leaker, Queenstown, 2006 (3rd edition).

First published in 1947 as part of a Southland Historical Committee project, this collection of reminiscences provides a unique account of life in early Martins Bay. Although never formally educated, Alice wrote charming stories that are detailed and quite matter-of-fact.

John Hall-Jones. *Martins Bay*. Craig Printing, Invercargill, 1987.
This comprehensive volume gives all the historical data of the Hollyford Valley from pre-European times through to the first explorers, the settlers of Jamestown, the McKenzies and Davey Gunn.

Greenstone and Caples Tracks
Barry Brailsford. *Greenstone Trails*. Reed, Wellington, 1984.
The most thorough exploration of the Maori views on pounamu, with fascinating details of legends, means of procurement and relevance to culture. The bulk of the text details the main trails used to trade the precious stone and as such makes inspirational reading for trampers who want a perspective on the Maori feet that have trodden these same tracks.

Russell J. Beck. *New Zealand Jade*. Reed, Wellington, 1984.
A good examination, from a mainly European and geological perspective, on jade and how it was collected, worked and used.

Rees–Dart Track
Neville Peat. *Land Aspiring*. Craig Potton, Nelson, 1995.
As with *Wild Fiordland*, Peat gives a comprehensive account of the natural and human histories of the Mt Aspiring region.

INDEX